p. 8
p. 96

MONOTHEISM AND MOSES

PROBLEMS IN EUROPEAN CIVILIZATION

MONOTHEISM AND MOSES

Edited with an introduction by

Robert J. Christen and Harold E. Hazelton

MANHATTAN COLLEGE

D. C. HEATH AND COMPANY
A DIVISION OF
RAYTHEON EDUCATION COMPANY
LEXINGTON, MASSACHUSETTS

Library of Congress Catalog Card Number: 68-8047

Printed in the United States of America

Table of Contents

IV. THE FREUDIAN HYPOTHESIS

V. THE HEBREW ORIGINS OF MONOTHEISM

Introduction

THE CULTURAL INFLUENCE of the Old Testament on European civilization is as incalculable as it is proverbial. Acknowledged over the centuries by Jews and Christians as Holy Writ, literally as the Word of God, the Old Testament has provided inspiration for many of Western man's noblest achievements, and, unfortunately, has been cited as justification for some of his darkest deeds.

The authorship of the sacred scriptures has been attributed traditionally to certain divinely inspired writers. Tradition has ascribed the first five books of the Old Testament, the Pentateuch, to Moses. Though obvious inconsistencies in the text had long troubled readers, the grip of the Mosaic tradition was so strong that through the centuries ingenious explanations were devised in its support. Not until the nineteenth century did biblical scholars succeed in probing into the question of authorship in a spirit of independent inquiry. At that time not only did they reject the idea of Mosaic authorship, but they also concluded that the Pentateuch had been compiled or edited from older oral and written sources by a number of persons. They also proved that the Pentateuch took final form only after the composition of many of the books in the Old Testament which follow it.

For a time, these discoveries prompted some scholars to dismiss the Pentateuch as historically worthless, but later findings by historians and archaeologists have reversed this trend. So many details of the biblical narrative have been proven correct that most authorities are convinced today that the early accounts of the patriarchal period (Abraham to Jacob) and of the Mosaic period are grounded on a solid substratum of fact. On the other hand, many believe that the editors of the Pentateuch made significant alterations in narrating the religious traditions from earlier times, in order to make the scriptures correspond more closely to their own beliefs and practices. In fact, there is evidence to suggest that the early Hebrews had much more in common with their Near Eastern neighbors, and were culturally more indebted to them, than was once supposed.

On many issues of Old Testament history, Jewish and Christian scholars, as well as those with no particular religious commitments, are in accord. But one issue that has given rise to widely differing interpretations and some very heated controversy is the genesis of Judaic monotheism. Once uncritically accepted as the most distinctive characteristic of the religious thought of the Jews — clearly discernible in the patriarchal period and emphatically proclaimed in the Mosaic era — monotheism, some scholars now insist, did not originate with the Hebrews and was not even explicitly embraced by them until long after the time of Moses. Monotheism is deceptively simple as a religious concept. It remains, however, a most complex historical problem. This volume presents conflicting hypotheses by renowned scholars about such questions as when monotheism gained acceptance by the Jews, whether Moses was a true monotheist, and what influence the alleged monotheism of the pharaoh Akhnaton may have had upon the religious history of the Jews.

Since the touchstone for any discussion of Judaic monotheism is still the Old Testament, our first selection is comprised of some especially pertinent passages from the

Book of Exodus. The first passage describes the oppression of the Hebrews at the hands of the Egyptians; the next, the rise of Moses as the deliverer of the Hebrews; and the last, the sojourn of the Hebrews at Sinai where Moses received the commandment: "I, the Lord, am your God, who brought you out of the land of Egypt, out of a state of slavery. You must have no other gods beside me."

The intellectual and ethical import of this famous injunction is the subject of the three selections in Part II. In the first, H. and H. A. Frankfort point out that the adoption of monotheism involved much more than the simple renunciation of "other gods." It signalled a qualitative change from previous patterns of thought about God's relationship to nature and to man. For example, the God of Israel imposed upon his subjects a moral standard which was simply not included in the religious thought of their polytheistic predecessors or neighbors. This point is illustrated in selections from the writings of Alexander Heidel and Stewart C. Easton. Heidel compares the familiar biblical flood story with its parallel from the literature of ancient Babylon. The two stories are strikingly similar in certain details, but Heidel argues that the moral dissimilarities are actually more pronounced. Easton offers additional reasons for regarding Jewish monotheism as a force for moral revolution.

Because Judaic monotheism is so important a development in human history, scholars have been especially interested in determining when and where the idea originated, and just how it was transmitted and refined. One hypothesis that has attracted considerable attention is that Judaic monotheism was inspired by the religious conceptions of the heretic king of Egypt, Akhnaton. The merits of this hypothesis, and some of its ramifications, are discussed in the selections grouped together in Part III, "The Egyptian Question." In the first selection, a famous American Egyptologist, James H. Breasted, unfolds his reasons for believing that Akhnaton, not Moses, was

the first true monotheist. Breasted did not claim that Akhnaton's faith, Atonism, influenced Moses, but he was convinced that Atonism had some impact upon the later religious development of the Jews. Breasted often cited in support of his position an apparent similarity between Akhnaton's hymn to Aton and the 104th Psalm. In the selection that follows, John A. Wilson acknowledges this similarity but accounts for it quite differently, thus reducing its significance. Moreover, he challenges the very notion that Akhnaton was a true monotheist.

Well before Wilson penned his criticisms, Sigmund Freud seized upon Breasted's claim that Akhnaton was the first monotheist and used it as an historical underpinning in *Moses and Monotheism,* the last of his celebrated writings on the nature of religious belief. In *Moses and Monotheism* Freud, who believed that the insights derived from psychoanalysis could be effectively employed to illuminate episodes lying beyond the purview of ordinary historians, put forth a startling hypothesis. Freud contended, contrary to what the Bible indicates, that Moses was not a Hebrew but an Egyptian disciple of Akhnaton who, following his master's death, adopted the Hebrews then in Egypt as his people, and initiated them into the Aton religion as he led them toward the promised land. Part IV, "The Freudian Hypothesis," includes a careful recapitulation and historical critiques of Freud's argument in complementary reviews of *Moses and Monotheism* by Salo Baron and H. L. Philp.[1] In a selection from Bruce Mazlish's provocative study, *The Riddle of History: The Great Speculators from Vico to Freud,* the reader will find a further evaluation of Freud's ideas in terms of his philosophy of history.

Whatever Mosaic religion owed to Egypt, there is no gainsaying that it was deeply indebted to the Hebrew patriarchs. The final section of the pamphlet opens with a

[1] Readers interested in examining Freud's writings on religion will find his major titles listed in the "Suggestions for Additional Reading."

discussion by Harry M. Orlinsky of the relationship between Abraham's and Moses' concepts of God and the covenant. This is followed by the first of two selections from the work of an American biblical scholar, William F. Albright, who affirms the idea that Moses was a genuine monotheist. The following selection is a strongly stated refutation of Albright's case: Theophile J. Meek, a Canadian biblical scholar, scorns Albright's view that Mosaic monotheism was part of a general trend toward monotheism in the Middle East. In fact, he rejects out of hand the claim that Moses was a monotheist, insisting that monotheism could not have developed among the Jews until well after Moses' time. A brief second selection from Albright serves as a rejoinder to Meek. This is followed by an essay by H. H. Rowley, a British biblical scholar, who takes a mediating position on the question of Mosaic monotheism. Rowley's essay reviews a number of other suggestions which have been advanced to explain the rise of monotheism in general, and Judaic monotheism in particular. He explains the "Kenite hypothesis," of which he is a leading advocate and rejects attempts to explain monotheism as a product of historical evolution from polytheism.

In contrast to Albright, Meek, and Rowley, who did not hesitate to use extra-biblical sources when writing about Moses, the famous Jewish scholar Martin Buber pointedly dismissed sources outside of the biblical narrative as not "worthy of serious consideration" in the preparation of his book, *Moses: The Revelation and the Covenant.*

Moreover, he refused to enter into the debate on the question of whether or not Moses was a monotheist. Indeed, Buber dismissed the term "monotheism" as a philosophical abstraction devoid of religious value. "What is important for us about this God of Moses," he said, "is the association of qualities and activities which is peculiar to Him." The selection from Buber's *Moses* demonstrates just what can be learned about the nature of Yahweh, as Moses called his God, from a close study of the *Old Testament.*

The concluding selection in this volume provides the reader with an overall summary of the development of the religious thought which finds expression in the Old Testament. This summary is taken from a monumental study, *The Rise of the West,* by William H. McNeill. Professor McNeill speaks of the interaction between religious and political developments which figured so greatly in shaping Judaism. He explains how the Jewish religion was able to take on a life of its own and to survive in independence of any particular locality or secular culture.

The selections reproduced in this volume are printed without the footnotes which originally buttressed them, except where needed to explain the text. Readers should familiarize themselves with the terms in the "Glossary" and the dates in the "Chronological Table" before reading the selections. Those who would like to read more about the origins of Judaic monotheism and related topics will find the "Suggestions for Additional Reading" useful.

CHRONOLOGICAL TABLE

EGYPT

The Old Kingdom (Pyramid Age)	2700–2200 B.C.
The First Intermediate Period	2200–2050
The Middle Kingdom (Feudal Age)	2050–1800
The Second Intermediate Period	1800–1550
The New Kingdom (The Empire)	1550–1090
Thutmose III	1468–1436
Amenhotep III	1398–1361
Akhnaton (Amenhotep IV)	1369–1353
Ramases II	1290–1224

ISRAEL

Abraham	possibly somewhere between 1900 and 1750 B.C.
The Exodus	probably between 1290 and 1250
Joshua and the Conquest of Palestine	1250–1200
King Saul	1020–1000
The United Monarchy	1000–922
King David	1000–961
King Solomon	961–922
The Divided Monarchy	922–587

JUDAH		ISRAEL	
		King Jeroboam I	922–901
		King Ahab	869–850
		Elijah	*fl.* 860–849
		King Jehu	842–815
		Amos	*fl.* 752–738
Isaiah	*fl.* 742–688	*Hosea*	*fl.* 746–735
		Fall of Israel	722/1
King Manasseh	687/6–642		
King Josiah	640/609		
Deuteronomic Reformation	622		
Jeremiah	*fl.* 627–582		
Fall of Judah	587		
Exile	587–538		
Deutero-Isaiah	*fl.* 547–538		
Cyrus's Decree of Restoration	538		

The earlier the dates, the more uncertain they are. Dates for persons or events in the 3rd and 2nd millenia B.C., as given in older works such as Breasted's, are now felt to be exaggerated and have often been reduced by a century or two. However, disagreement still flourishes. The editors have rather arbitrarily followed John A. Wilson for Egyptian dates and in most cases John Bright for those concerning Israel. The terminal dates given above for the preaching of the prophets are quite uncertain and in most cases are meant only to mark off the approximate time of their activity.

GLOSSARY

ADAD, HADAD   A Semitic god of storm and rain worshiped from Mesopotamia to Canaan (Palestine). In Phoenicia and Canaan he was usually known as *Ba'al*, a title (not a name) meaning Lord. See *Shaddai*.

AKHNATON, AKHENATEN, AKH-EN-ATON, IKHNATON.   In the sixth year of his reign Pharaoh Amenhotep IV changed his name to Akh-en-Aton (He-who-is-serviceable-to-the-Aton) and replaced the worship of *Amon-Re* and almost all the other Egyptian gods with the worship of himself and *Aton*.

AMON, AMEN, AMUN   The Egyptian god of air and the patron of Thebes. When Thebes became the capital of Egypt in the Middle Kingdom, Amon was syncretized with *Re*, the supreme deity of the Old Kingdom, as *Amon-Re*. See *Re*.

ANU   The Mesopotamian sky god and father of the gods.

ANNUNNAKI   The Mesopotamian divine judges of the underworld.

APODICTIC LAW   Unconditional, absolute law, stated in terse language, e.g. "Thou shalt not kill." In contrast to their *casuistic law*, the Jews' apodictic law is more narrowly concerned with ritual or ethics.

ATON, ATEN   The Egyptian name for the physical disk of the sun, which became a symbol of the deified, life-sustaining force which the sun exerts on the earth. See *Akhenaten*.

ATRAHASIS   "The exceedingly wise"; another name for *Utnapishtim*.

BA'AL   See *Adad*.

CASUISTIC LAW   Conditional or case law, introduced by a conditional clause, e.g. "If a thief is found breaking in, and if he is struck and dies, there shall be no blood guilt for him." It is among Jewish laws of this type that clauses borrowed from earlier Gentile law codes are to be found. Jewish casuistic law tended to be more concerned with what we today would consider civil and criminal law.

CORPORATIVE   Tending to consider all animate things, both human and divine, as not having strong individual personalites and as merging into a collective or corporate personality. Egyptian *monophysitism* (which see) is a later manifestation of this tendency of primitive thought.

Early Semitic alphabets contained only symbols for consonants. Depending on tradition and context the reader supplied vowels to complete the word. (For example, "pnd" might be "pond" or "pound.") The result has been uncertainty today about the spelling and pronunciation of Hebrew words, and some disputes about their meanings. See the footnote on p. 60 and the term "Yahweh" in this glossary [Editor's note].

D, DEUTERONOMIST See *documentary hypothesis.* The Deuteronomists or Deuteronomic school were a Judean group in the 7th century B.C. dedicated to the purification and revival of Judaism. They won King Josiah to their purpose and during his reign "discovered" a forgotten version of the Mosaic law which was probably the core of the present Book of Deuteronomy.

DEUTERO-ISAIAH, SECOND ISAIAH A prophet of the 6th century B.C., possibly of the same name as the earlier prophet Isaiah (late 8th c.), whose writing was appended to Isaiah's.

DOCUMENTARY HYPOTHESIS A proposal by 19th c. *higher criticism* (which see) that there were four documents of varying dates and places of composition from which was compiled the Pentateuch (the first five books of the Bible). The four documents are known as the J or *Yahwist,* the E or *Elohist,* the D or *Deuteronomist,* and the P or *Priestly.* The hypothesis, in modified form, is almost universally accepted today.

DYNAMISTIC Based on sympathetic magic, a primitive practice in which enactment of the correct ritual will allow the human participant to control a force or divinity (whom he often imitates in the ritual) for his own benefit.

E, ELOHIST See *documentary hypothesis.*

EA, ENKI The Mesopotamian god of fresh water and wisdom.

EL The Phoenician and Canaanite father god and nominal head of the pantheon. Perhaps originally the sky god, he was remote and inactive, *Ba'al* being the effective chief god. The Phoenician name was originally a common noun meaning "god" and continued to be used as a surrogate for the names of different gods. Phoenician and Hebrew being closely related tongues, the Jews used the plural form (*Elohim*) as an appellation for *Yahweh,* to stress his unity and universality, and it is thus translated "God."

ENLIL The Mesopotamian god of storm and violence.

HELIOPOLIS "City of the sun," the Greek name for On, the Egyptian city which housed the chief temple and priesthood of *Re.*

HENOTHEISM The worship and emphasis of one god by the *absorption* of other gods. This term is often used by many scholars, including Rowley, as synonymous with monolatry, but Meek stresses the distinction noted here. See *monolatry.*

HIGHER CRITICISM The literary and historical study of the Bible which seeks to discover the author, date, place of composition, and historical value of each text, as well as the meaning intended by the author. It is distinguished from lower or textual criticism, which seeks to establish the authentic text.

IRRA The Mesopotamian god of pestilence.

IRRAGAL Another name for Nergal, the Mesopotamian god of the underworld.

ISHTAR, LADY OF THE GODS   The Mesopotamian goddess of love and female fertility.

J OR YAHWIST   See *documentary hypothesis*.

KENITES   A clan of the Midianite tribe which lived east of the Gulf of Aqaba adjoining the peninsula of Sinai.

MA'AT   A unique Egyptian concept whose most basic meaning is the divine order of the universe. It can therefore also mean truth or justice, depending on the context.

MONOLATRY   The worship and emphasis of one god by the *exclusion* of others, without denying their existence.

MONOPHYSITISM   As applied to the ancient Egyptian religion, the belief that while there are many gods and many men, they are all ultimately of one nature. This consubstantiality permits a very fluid exchange or substitution of beings, e.g. the merging of gods, men becoming gods after death, and rulers (pharaohs) living as gods in human form.

NINURTA   The Mesopotamian god of war, and of wells and irrigation works.

OSIRIS   The Egyptian god of life after death, king of the land of the reborn dead, and, when a conception of the last judgment arose, the divine judge.

PRACTICAL MONOTHEISM   A phrase often used as a synonym for *monolatry,* in the sense that monolatry is monotheism in practice. It is contrasted to theoretical or pure monotheism, which denies explicitly the existence of other gods.

RE, RA   The Egyptian sun god and head of the pantheon. In the Middle Kingdom he was fused with Amon, the god of air, to form Amon-Re.

SECOND ISAIAH   See *Deutero-Isaiah*.

SHADDAI, EL SHADDAI   A god, possibly the chief god of the early Hebrew patriarchs; the name was later applied to *Yahweh* as an epithet. One etymology, "The One of the Mountains," depicts the original Shaddai as an equivalent to *Ba'al* of the Canaanites or *Adad* of the Semites in general. However, since another etymology derives from the word "power," the term (when applied to Yahweh in the Old Testament) is traditionally translated "God Almighty" (Gen. 17:1; 43:14; Ex. 6:3).

SKEUMORPHISM   A basic archaeological principle whereby change of material is accompanied by minimum change of form, e.g. the change of Greek temples from wood and terra cotta construction to marble with almost no change of architectural form.

UTNAPISHTIM   The Mesopotamian Noah. In the *Epic of Gilgamesh* he recounts the story of the flood to his descendant, the hero Gilgamesh. See *Atraḫasis*.

YAHWEH, JAHWEH, YAHWE, YHWH, YHVH   The personal name given to the god proclaimed by Moses.

The Conflict of Opinion

"It is possible to detect the reflection of Egyptian and Mesopotamian beliefs in many episodes of the Old Testament; but the overwhelming impression left by that document is one, not of derivation, but of originality."

—— H. AND H. A. FRANKFORT

". . . the monotheism long ago implicit in the teaching of the priests of Heliopolis, was . . . given unequivocal expression by Ikhnaton."

—— JAMES HENRY BREASTED

"The most important observation about Amarna religion is that there were two gods central to the faith, and not one. Akh-en-Aton and his family worshipped the Aton, and everybody else worshipped Akh-en Aton *as a god*."

—— JOHN A. WILSON

"The well-known lack of agreement among modern biblical scholars and anthropologists on some of the most fundamental issues . . . equips the analytical investigator with a mass of alternative suggestions from which he may choose those which best fit into the pattern of his theory. 'The more shadowy tradition has become,' says Freud, 'the more meet is it for the poet's use.' . . . Nevertheless, perhaps as a result of being too much earth-bound and source-bound, the present reviewer feels that he cannot quite follow the author into this rarefied atmosphere of pure speculation."

—— SALO W. BARON

"Facts of history, sound anthropology, convincing psychology in relation to the racial unconscious, evidence worthy of serious consideration or even solid argument — none of these is prominent in [Freud's] *Moses and Monotheism*."

—— H. L. PHILP

"The *Moses* thesis is hard either to prove or to disprove. The events which it claims to explain are buried under the swirl of time, and there is little clear documentary evidence surviving. . . . We can only conclude, therefore, that Freud's application of psychoanalytic insights to the traditional accounts of the origins of the Jewish and Christian religions results merely in a tenuous connection with what is, to begin with, unsatisfactory empirical data. The Moses book is indeed a very speculative work in the philosophy of history. What remains from Freud's work here is a chain of great "ifs," and a number of ingenious suggestions."

—— BRUCE MAZLISH

"It would be going too far to attribute to the patriarchal Hebrews a belief in the existence of one and only one God. In a sense they may be said to have practiced — but without defining — monotheism."

—— HARRY M. ORLINSKY

"Was Moses a true monotheist? If . . . the term 'monotheist' means one who teaches the existence of only one God, the creator of everything, the source of justice, who is equally powerful in Egypt, in the desert, and in Palestine, who has no sexuality and no mythology, who is human in form but cannot be seen by human eye and cannot be respresented in any form — then the founder of Yahwism was certainly a monotheist."

—— WILLIAM FOXWELL ALBRIGHT

"Albright protests against giving a unitarian definition to the word 'monotheism,' but the only acceptable use of the word is in its dictionary sense, and it is Albright and his kind, rather than his opponents, as he affirms, who are 'highly misleading' when they read into a word a meaning it cannot and should not bear."

—— THEOPHILE JAMES MEEK

". . . no evidence can be provided to show that polytheism developed into monotheism in Israel by natural evolution or by philosophic speculation. There is no evidence that Moses was a polytheist in the sense that he practised the worship of many gods; yet there is no evidence that he was a monotheist in the sense that he denied the existence of more than one God. Yahweh was to be the only God for Israel, and Him only were they to serve."

—— H. H. ROWLEY

"In order to learn at first hand who Moses was and the kind of life that was his, it is obviously necessary to study the Biblical narrative. There are no other sources worthy of serious consideration."

—— MARTIN BUBER

"By 500 B.C., the religion of Yahweh had undergone far-reaching transformations that fitted it to survive as a world religion. Judaism was no longer the cult of a tribe, as in the days of Moses, but a law and doctrine claiming universal validity for itself and total error for all rivals. . . . Judaism retained a strong emphasis upon the concept of a chosen people . . . ; yet within this collective and corporate frame there developed a belief in direct personal accountancy to God for individual moral and ritual acts."

—— WILLIAM H. McNEILL

I. THE PRIMARY SOURCE

Exodus

Exodus is the second of the five books of the Pentateuch. The translation by Theophile J. Meek, from which the following excerpts have been taken, is regarded as one of the most accurate.

THE FOLLOWING are the names of the sons of Israel who came to Egypt in the company of Jacob, each with his household: Reuben, Simeon, Levi, and Judah, Issachar, Zebulun, and Benjamin, Dan and Naphtali, Gad and Asher. The total number of persons that were direct descendants of Jacob was seventy, Joseph being already in Egypt. Then Joseph died, and likewise all his brothers and all that generation; but the Israelites were fruitful and prolific; they increased in numbers, and grew greater and greater, so that the land was filled with them.

Then a new king rose over Egypt, who knew nothing about Joseph; he said to his people,

"See, the Israelite people have become too numerous and too strong for us; come, let us take precautions against them lest they become so numerous that in the case of a war they should join forces with our enemies and fight against us, and so escape from the land."

Accordingly, gang-foremen were put in charge of them, to oppress them with their heavy labor; and they built Pithom and Raamses as store-cities for Pharaoh. But the more they oppressed them, the more they multiplied and expanded, so that they became apprehensive about the Israelites.

The Egyptians reduced the Israelites to rigorous slavery; they made life bitter for them in hard work with mortar and bricks, and in all kinds of work in the fields, all the work that they exacted of them being rigorous.

Then the king of Egypt spoke to the midwives attending the Hebrew women, of whom the name of one was Shiphrah and that of the other Puah.

"When you act as midwives for the Hebrew women," he said, "you are to look at the genitals; if it is a boy, you must kill him, but if it is a girl, she may live."

But the midwives stood in awe of God, and so did not do as the king of Egypt told them, but let the male children live. So the king of Egypt summoned the midwives, and said to them,

"Why have you done this: let the male children live?"

The midwives said to Pharaoh,

"Because the Hebrew women are not like the Egyptian women; but are animals, in that they are delivered before the midwife reaches them!"

So God was good to the midwives; the people multiplied and grew very numerous, and because the midwives stood in awe of God, they established families for them.

So Pharaoh commanded all his people,

Reprinted from *The Old Testament: An American Translation* edited by J. M. Powis Smith, pp. 92–97, 122–125, 130–131, by permission of The University of Chicago Press. Copyright 1927 by The University of Chicago.

"Every boy that is born to the Hebrews, you must throw into the Nile, but you are to let all the girls live."

2 Now a man belonging to the house of Levi went and married a daughter of Levi. The woman conceived and bore a son, and seeing that he was robust, she hid him for three months. When she could no longer hide him, she procured an ark of papyrus reeds for him, and daubing it with bitumen and pitch, she put the child in it, and placed it among the reeds beside the bank of the Nile. His sister posted herself some distance away to see what would happen to him.

Presently Pharaoh's daughter came down to bathe at the Nile, while her maids walked on the bank of the Nile. Then she saw the ark among the reeds and sent her maid to get it. On opening it, she saw the child, and it was a boy crying! She took pity on him, and said,

"This is one of the Hebrews' children."

Thereupon his sister said to Pharaoh's daughter,

"Shall I go and summon a nurse for you from the Hebrew women, to nurse the child for you?"

"Go," said Pharaoh's daughter to her.

So the girl went and called the child's mother, to whom Pharaoh's daughter said,

"Take this child away and nurse it for me, and I will pay the wages due you."

So the woman took the child and nursed him; and when the child grew up, she brought him to Pharaoh's daughter, and he became her son. She called his name Moses [drawn out]; "For," said she, "I drew him out of the water."

It was in those days that Moses, now grown up, went out to visit his fellow-countrymen and noted their heavy labor. He saw an Egyptian kill a Hebrew, one of his own countrymen; so, looking this way and that, and seeing that there was no one in sight, he killed the Egyptian, and hid him in the sand. Another day, when he went out, there were two Hebrews fighting! So he said to him that was in the wrong,

"Why do you strike your companion?"

He replied,

"Who made you ruler and judge over us? Are you thinking of murdering me as you did the Egyptian?"

Then was Moses afraid. "The incident must surely be known," he thought.

When Pharaoh heard about the matter, he tried to kill Moses, but Moses fled from Pharaoh and went to the land of Midian, and sat down beside a well.

Now the priest of Midian had seven daughters, who came to draw water, and fill the troughs to water their father's flock, but some shepherds came and drove them off. So Moses went to their rescue and watered their flock. When they came home to their father Reuel, he said,

"How did you come to get home so soon today?"

They said,

"An Egyptian protected us against the shepherds; he even drew water for us, and watered the flock."

"Then where is he?" he said to his daughters. "Why did you leave the man behind? Invite him to have a meal."

When Moses agreed to live with the man, he gave Moses his daughter Zipporah in marriage; and she bore a son, whom he named Gershom [immigrant]; "For," said he, "I am an immigrant in a foreign land."

In the course of this long time the king of Egypt died. The Israelites, groaning under their bondage, cried for help, and their cry because of their bondage came up to God. God heard their moaning, and God remembered his covenant with Abraham, Isaac, and Jacob; God saw the plight of Israel, and took cognizance of it.

3 While Moses was tending the flock of his father-in-law, Jethro, the priest of Midian, he led the flock to the western side of the desert, and came to the mountain of God, Horeb. Then the angel of the LORD appeared to him in a flame of fire, rising out of a bush. He looked, and there was the bush burning with fire without being consumed! So Moses said,

"I will turn aside and see this great sight, why the bush is not burned up."

When the Lord saw that he had turned aside to look at it, God called to him out of the bush.

"Moses, Moses!" he said.

"Here I am!" said he.

"Do not come near here," he said; "take your sandals off your feet; for the place on which you are standing is holy ground."

"I am the God of your father," he said, "the God of Abraham, Isaac, and Jacob."

Then Moses hid his face; for he was afraid to look at God.

"I have indeed seen the plight of my people who are in Egypt," the Lord said, "and I have heard their cry under their oppressors; for I know their sorrows, and I have come down to rescue them from the Egyptians and bring them up out of that land to a land, fine and large, to a land abounding in milk and honey, to the country of the Canaanites, Hittites, Amorites, Perizzites, Hivvites, and Jebusites. Now the cry of the Israelites has reached me, and I have also seen how the Egyptians are oppressing them; so come now, let me send you to Pharaoh, that you may bring my people, the Israelites, out of Egypt."

But Moses said to God,

"Who am I, to go to Pharaoh and bring the Israelites out of Egypt?"

"I will be with you," he said; "and this shall be the sign for you that I have sent you. When you bring the people out of Egypt, you shall serve God at this mountain."

"But," said Moses to God, "in case I go to the Israelites and say to them, 'The God of your fathers has sent me to you,' and they say to me, 'What is his name?' what am I to say to them?"

"I am who I am," God said to Moses. Then he said, "This is what you are to say to the Israelites: '"I am" has sent me to you.'"

God said further to Moses,

"This is what you are to say to the Israelites: 'The Lord, the God of your fathers, the God of Abraham, Isaac, and Jacob, has sent me to you.' This is my name for all time, and this is my title for age after age. Go and assemble the elders of Israel, and say to them, 'The Lord, the God of your fathers, the God of Abraham, Isaac, and Jacob, has appeared to me, saying, "I have given careful heed to you and your treatment in Egypt, and I have resolved to bring you up out of your tribulation in Egypt to the land of the Canaanites, Hittites, Amorites, Perizzites, Hivvites, and Jebusites, to a land abounding in milk and honey."' They will heed your appeal; and then you and the elders of Israel shall come to the king of Egypt and say to him, 'The Lord, the God of the Hebrews, has paid us a visit; so now, let us make a three days' journey into the desert to offer sacrifices to the Lord our God.' I know, however, that the king of Egypt will not let you go without the use of force; so I will stretch out my hand and smite Egypt with all the marvels that I shall perform in it; after that he will let you go. And I will bring this people into such favor with the Egyptians that you shall not go away empty-handed when you do leave; each woman must ask her neighbor and the guest in her home for articles of silver and gold, and for clothing, which you are to put on your sons and daughters. Thus shall you despoil the Egyptians."

4 "But suppose they will not believe me," answered Moses, "nor heed my plea, but say, 'The Lord did not appear to you.'"

The Lord said to him,

"What have you in your hand?"

"A staff," he said.

"Throw it on the ground," said he.

He threw it on the ground, and it became a snake. Moses ran away from it, but the Lord said to Moses,

"Stretch out your hand and lay hold of its tail" — stretching out his hand, he seized it, and it became a staff in his hand — "in order that they may be convinced that the Lord, the God of their fathers, did appear to you, the God of Abraham, Isaac, and Jacob."

The Lord said further to him,

"Put your hand into your bosom."

He put his hand into his bosom, and

when he took it out, there was his hand leprous, as white as snow!

"Put your hand back into your bosom," he said.

He put his hand back into his bosom, and when he took it out of his bosom, there it was, like the rest of his body again.

"If they will not believe you, nor accept the evidence of the first sign, they may acknowledge the evidence of the second. If they will not be convinced by even these two signs, nor heed your plea, you are to take some water from the Nile and pour it on the dry ground; and the water that you take from the Nile shall become blood on the dry ground."

But Moses said to the LORD,

"Pray, O Lord, I have been no speaker, neither in the past nor recently, nor since thou hast spoken to thy servant; but I am slow of speech and slow of tongue."

The LORD said to him,

"Who gives man a mouth, or makes him dumb, or deaf, or lame, or blind? Is it not I, the LORD? Now go; I will help you to speak, and will instruct you what to say."

But he said,

"Pray, O Lord, commission whom thou wilt."

Then the anger of the LORD blazed against Moses, and he said,

"Is there not your brother Aaron, the Levite? I know that he is a ready speaker, and further, he is just coming out to meet you, and will be overjoyed at seeing you. You must speak to him, and put the words in his mouth; I will help both you and him to speak, and I will instruct you both what to do. He shall speak for you to the people; he shall serve as a mouthpiece for you, and you shall act the part of God to him. You must take this staff in your hand, with which to perform the signs."

Then Moses went off, and returning to his father-in-law Jethro, said to him,

"Pray let me go back to my relatives in Egypt, to see whether they are still living."

"Go in peace," said Jethro to Moses.

The LORD said to Moses in Midian,

"Go, return to Egypt; for all the men who sought your life are dead."

So Moses took his wife and sons, and mounted them on asses, to return to the land of Egypt; Moses also took the staff of God in his hand.

The LORD said to Moses,

"When you return to Egypt, see that you perform before Pharaoh all the portents which I have put in your power; but I will make him obstinate, so that he will not let the people go. You are to say to Pharaoh, 'Thus says the LORD: "Israel is my firstborn son; so I said to you, 'Let my son go, that he may serve me;' but you refused to let him go; accordingly I am going to slay your first-born son."'"

At a camping place in the course of the journey the LORD encountered him, and tried to kill him. So Zipporah took a flint, and cutting off her son's foreskin, she touched his person with it, saying,

"You are my bridegroom in blood."

Then he let him alone.

* * *

19 On the third new moon after leaving the land of Egypt, on that very day the Israelites entered the desert of Sinai. Setting out from Rephidim, they entered the desert of Sinai, and camped in the desert; Israel camped there in front of the mountain, while Moses went up to God. Then the LORD called to him from the mountain, saying,

"Thus shall you say to the house of Jacob, and tell the Israelites: 'You have seen for yourselves what I did to the Egyptians, and how I bore you on eagles' wings, and brought you to myself. Now then, if you will but heed my injunctions, and keep my covenant, you shall be my very own out of all the peoples (for all the earth is mine), and you shall be a kingdom of priests to me, and a holy nation.' These are the words that you are to speak to the Israelites."

So Moses came and summoned all the elders of the people, and set before them all these words which the LORD had commanded him. Then the people all answered together,

"Whatever the Lord says we will do."

And Moses reported the words of the people to the Lord.

The Lord said to Moses,

"See, I am coming to you in a thick cloud, in order that the people may hear me speaking with you, and may then always trust you too."

When Moses reported the words of the people to the Lord, the Lord said to Moses,

"Go to the people, and have them go through a period of consecration today and tomorrow; let them wash their clothes, and be ready by the day after tomorrow; for on the day after tomorrow the Lord is going to descend on Mount Sinai in sight of all the people. You must mark off the mountain all around, saying, 'Take care not to ascend the mountain, nor even to touch the edge of it; whoever touches the mountain must be put to death, having no hand touch him, but being stoned or shot; whether it is man or beast, he shall not be allowed to live. When a long blast is blown on the ram's horn, they may come up to the mountain.'"

So Moses descended from the mountain to the people; he consecrated the people, and they washed their clothes.

"Be ready by the day after tomorrow," he said to the people; "approach no woman."

On the third day, when morning came, there was thunder and lightning, with a heavy cloud over the mountain, and a very loud trumpet-blast, so that all the people that were in the camp trembled. Then Moses brought the people out of the camp to meet God, and they took their stand at the foot of the mountain. Mount Sinai was completely enveloped in smoke, because the Lord had descended upon it in fire; its smoke ascended like the smoke from a kiln, so that the people all trembled violently. As the blast of the trumpet grew louder and louder, Moses spoke, and God answered him with a thunderpeal. The Lord descended upon Mount Sinai, to the top of the mountain; the Lord then summoned Moses to the top of the mountain, and when Moses went up, the Lord said to Moses,

"Go down and warn the people not to break through to the Lord to see him, or many of them will fall. The priests, also, whose place it is to approach the Lord, are to sanctify themselves, lest the Lord break loose upon them."

Moses said to the Lord,

"The people may not come up to Mount Sinai; for thou thyself didst charge us, saying, 'Mark off the mountain, and make it taboo.'"

The Lord said to him,

"Go down, and then come up again, accompanied by Aaron; but the priests and the people are not to break through to come up to the Lord, lest he break loose upon them."

So Moses went down to the people, and told them.

20 God spoke all these words, saying,

① "I, the Lord, am your God, who brought you out of the land of Egypt, out of a state of slavery. You must have no other gods beside me.

"You must not carve an image for yourself in the shape of anything that is in the heavens above, or that is on the earth below, or that is in the waters under the earth; you must not pay homage to them, nor serve them; for I, the Lord your God, am a jealous God, punishing children for the sins of their fathers, to the third or fourth generation of those who hate me, but showing grace to the thousandth generation of those who love me and keep my commands.

② "You must not invoke the name of the Lord your God to evil intent; for the Lord will not excuse anyone who invokes his name to evil intent.

③ "Remember to keep the sabbath day holy. Six days you are to labor and do all your work, but on the seventh day, a sabbath to the Lord your God, you must not do any work at all, neither you, nor your son, nor your daughter, nor your male or female slave, nor your cattle, nor the alien in your employ residing in your community; for in six days the LORD made the heavens, the earth, and the sea, together with all that is in them, but rested on the seventh day; that is how the LORD came to bless the seventh day and to hallow it.

"Honor your father and mother, that you may live long in the land that the LORD your God is giving you.

"You must not commit murder.

"You must not commit adultery.

"You must not steal.

"You must not bring a false charge against your fellow.

"You must not covet your neighbor's home; you must not covet your neighbor's wife, nor his male or female slave, nor his ox, nor his ass, nor anything at all that is your neighbor's."

As the people all perceived the thunder and lightning, the blast of the trumpet, and the mountain smoking, the people became afraid, and fell back, standing off at a distance.

"If you yourself will speak to us," they said to Moses, "we will listen; but do not let God speak to us, lest we die."

"Fear not," said Moses to the people; "for it is only to test you that God has come, and in order that the fear of him may be present with you to keep you from sinning."

The people, however, stood off at a distance, while Moses approached the dense darkness where God was.

Then the LORD said to Moses,

"Thus shall you say to the Israelites: 'You have seen for yourselves that I have been talking with you out of the heavens. Gods of silver, and gods of gold you must not make for yourselves. You must construct an altar of earth for me, and sacrifice on it your burnt-offerings, your thank-offerings, your sheep, and your oxen; at every sanctuary where I record my name, I will come to you and bless you. If, however, you construct an altar of stones for me, you must not build it of dressed stones; for if you were to use your tools on it, you would pollute it. Further, you must never ascend my altar on steps, so that your nakedness may not be exposed on it.'

*   *   *

24 "Come up to the LORD," he said to Moses, "you, and Aaron, Nadab, Abihu, and seventy of the elders of Israel, and worship at a distance; Moses alone is to come near the LORD; the others are not to come near, nor are the people to go up with him."

Then Moses came, and recounted to the people all the regulations of the LORD and all the ordinances; and the people all answered with one voice,

"All the regulations that the LORD has given we will observe."

So Moses wrote down all the regulations of the LORD, and rising early next morning, he built an altar at the foot of the mountain, along with twelve sacred pillars, one for each of the twelve tribes of Israel. Then he sent the young men of the Israelites to offer burnt-offerings and to sacrifice oxen as thank-offerings to the LORD, while Moses himself took half of the blood, and put it in basins, dashing the other half on the altar. He then took the book of the covenant, and read it in the hearing of the people, who said,

"All that the LORD has directed we will obediently do."

Then Moses took the blood and dashed it on the people, saying,

"That is the blood of the covenant which the LORD has made with you on the basis of all these regulations."

Moses then went up, with Aaron, Nadab, Abihu, and seventy of the elders of Israel, and they saw the God of Israel, with something like a sapphire pavement under his feet, as clear as the sky itself. And God did not lay hands on the leaders of the Israelites, but they beheld God, and ate and drank.

The LORD said to Moses,

"Ascend the mountain to me, and be present there, that I may give you the stone tablets, with the instructions and commands that I have written on them for their instruction."

So Moses, with his attendant Joshua, rose; and Moses ascended the mountain of God, saying to the elders,

"Wait here for us until we come back to you. Aaron and Hur are here with you; whoever has a dispute may bring it to them."

So Moses ascended the mountain, while the cloud covered the mountain, and the glory of the Lord rested on Mount Sinai; for six days the cloud covered it, but on the seventh day he called to Moses from the midst of the cloud. The glory of the Lord looked to the Israelites like a consuming fire on the top of the mountain. Moses penetrated the cloud, and ascended the mountain; Moses remained on the mountain for forty days and nights.

II. THE SIGNIFICANCE OF MONOTHEISM

Emancipation from Myth

H. AND H. A. FRANKFORT

Archaeologist Henri Frankfort was born in Amsterdam, Holland in 1897. As a young man he led several archaeological expeditions in Egypt and Iraq. In 1932 he became Research Professor of Oriental Archaeology at the University of Chicago. From 1949 until his death in 1954, Frankfort served as Director of the Warburg Institute in London. His wife, who frequently assisted him in his work, is one of the coauthors of the following selection. Frankfort's writings include *Ancient Egyptian Religion, Art and Architecture of the Ancient Orient,* and *Kingship and the Gods.*

WHEN WE READ in Psalm 19 that "the heavens declare the glory of God; and the firmament sheweth his handiwork," we hear a voice which mocks the beliefs of Egyptians and Babylonians. The heavens, which were to the psalmist but a witness of God's greatness, were to the Mesopotamians the very majesty of godhead, the highest ruler, Anu. To the Egyptians the heavens signified the mystery of the divine mother through whom man was reborn. In Egypt and Mesopotamia the divine was comprehended as immanent: the gods were in nature. The Egyptians saw in the sun all that a man may know of the Creator; the Mesopotamians viewed the sun as the god Shamash, the guarantor of justice. But to the psalmist the sun was God's devoted servant who "is as a bridegroom coming out of his chamber, and rejoiceth as a strong man to run a race." The God of the psalmists and the prophets was not in nature. He transcended nature—and transcended, likewise, the realm of mythopoeic thought. It would seem that the He-brews, no less than the Greeks, broke with the mode of speculation which had prevailed up to their time.

The mainspring of the acts, thoughts, and feelings of early man was the conviction that the divine was immanent in nature, and nature intimately connected with society. [Some scholars have] emphasized this fact by calling the Egyptians monophysites [and] . . . Mesopotamian . . . myths and beliefs . . . reflect it at every turn. . . . The assumption of an essential correlation between nature and man provide[s] us with a basis for the understanding of mythopoeic thought. Its logic, its peculiar structure, [is] seen to derive from an unceasing awareness of a live relationship between man and the phenomenal world. In the significant moments of his life, early man was confronted not by an inanimate, impersonal nature—not by an "It"—but by a "Thou." We have seen that such a relationship involved not only man's intellect but the whole of his being—his feeling and his will, no less than his thought. Hence early man would have rejected the detachment of a purely intellectual attitude toward nature, had he been able to conceive it, as inadequate to his experience.

As long as the peoples of the ancient Near East preserved their cultural integrity — from the middle of the fourth to the middle of the first millennium B.C. — they remained conscious of their close bond with nature. And that awareness remained vivid notwithstanding the conditions of city life. The efflorescence of civilization in Egypt and Mesopotamia brought with it the need for a division of labor and a diversification of life possible only when people congregate in sufficient numbers for some to be freed from preoccupation with earning a livelihood. But the ancient cities were small by our standards, and their inhabitants were not cut off from the land. On the contrary, most of them derived their sustenance from the surrounding fields; all of them worshiped gods personifying natural powers; and all of them participated in rites which marked the turning-points in the farmer's year. In the great metropolis of Babylon the outstanding annual event was the New Year's Festival celebrating the renewal of the generative force of nature. In all Mesopotamian cities the business of everyday life was interrupted several times in the course of each month when the moon completed one of its phases or other natural events called for appropriate action on the part of the community. In Egypt, too, the husbandman's preoccupations found expression in festivals at Thebes, Memphis, and other Egyptian cities where celebrations marked the rise of the Nile, the end of the inundation, or the completion of the harvest. Thus urban life in no way diminished man's awareness of his essential involvement in nature.

When we accentuate the basic conception of ancient Near Eastern thought, as we have just done, we are necessarily obscuring its richness and diversity. Within the scope of mythopoeic thought a great variety of attitudes and outlooks are possible; and contrast as well as variety become

apparent when we compare the speculative myths of Egypt and Mesopotamia. It is true that the same natural phenomena were often personified in these two countries and that the same images were often used to describe them. Yet the mood of the myths and the significance of the images are most unlike.

In both countries, for instance, the existing world was believed to have emerged from the waters of chaos. In Egypt this primeval ocean was male — the god Nūn. In other words, it was conceived as a fertilizing agent, and as such it was a permanent factor in the created universe recognized in the subsoil water and in the annual flood of the Nile. In Mesopotamia the fertilizing power in water was personified as the god Enki or Ea. But he was entirely unrelated to the primordial ocean. This ocean was a female, Ti'amat, the mother who brought forth gods and monsters in such profusion that her unbounded fruitfulness endangered the very existence of the universe. She was killed in combat by Marduk, who formed the world from her body. Thus water was significant to both Babylonians and Egyptians as the source and also as the sustainer of life. Yet these conceptions were very differently expressed by the two peoples.

A similar contrast appears in relation to earth. Mesopotamia worshiped a beneficial Great Mother whose fertility was seen in the produce of the earth and who gained additional religious importance by a variety of associations. The earth was viewed as the counterpart (and hence the spouse) of Heaven, Anu; or of the waters, Enki; or even of Enlil, the kingly storm-god. In Egypt, on the other hand, the earth was a male — Geb or Ptah or Osiris: the ubiquitous mother-goddess was not connected with the soil. Her image was either cast in the primitive and ancient guise of the cow or projected on the sky which, as Nūt, gave birth to the sun and stars each day at dawn and dusk. Moreover, the dead entered her body to be reborn as immortals. The sustained Egyptian preoccupation with death and the hereafter, however, found no equivalent in Mesopotamia. On the contrary, death was understood there as an almost complete destruction of personality; and man's chief desires were for a worthy life and freedom from disease, with a good reputation and descendants to survive him; and the sky was not a goddess bending over her children but the most unapproachable of male gods.

The differences which we have enumerated do not merely represent a meaningless variety of images; they betray a thorough contrast between the Egyptian and Mesopotamian views as to the nature of the universe in which man lives. Throughout the Mesopotamian texts we hear overtones of anxiety which seem to express a haunting fear that the unaccountable and turbulent powers may at any time bring disaster to human society. But in Egypt the gods were powerful without being violent. Nature presented itself as an established order in which changes were either superficial and insignificant or an unfolding in time of what had been preordained from the beginning. Moreover, Egyptian kingship guaranteed stability to society. For . . . one of the gods occupied the throne. Pharaoh was divine, the son and image of the Creator. Thus Pharaoh insured a harmonious integration of nature and society at all times. But in Mesopotamia the assembly of the gods assigned a mere mortal to rule men, and the divine favor might at any time be withdrawn from him. Man was at the mercy of decisions he could neither influence nor gauge. Hence the king and his counselors watched for portents on earth and in the sky which might reveal a changing constellation of divine grace, so that catastrophe might be foreseen and possibly averted. In Egypt neither astrology nor prophecy ever developed to any great extent.

The contrast between the temper of the two countries was concisely expressed in their creation myths. In Egypt creation was viewed as the brilliant act of an omnipotent Creator disposing of submissive elements. Of the lasting order which he created, society formed an unchanging part. In Mesopotamia the Creator had been chosen by a divine assembly helpless before the threat of the powers of chaos. Their champion, Marduk, had followed up his victory over these antagonists by the creation of the universe. This took place almost as an afterthought, and man was especially designed as a servant of the gods. There was no permanence in the human sphere. The gods assembled on every New Year's Day to "establish (such) destinies" for mankind as they pleased.

The differences between the Egyptian and Mesopotamian manners of viewing the world are very far-reaching. Yet the two peoples agreed in the fundamental assumptions that the individual is part of society, that society is imbedded in nature, and that nature is but the manifestation of the divine. This doctrine was, in fact, universally accepted by the peoples of the ancient world with the single exception of the Hebrews.

The Hebrews arrived late upon the scene and settled in a country pervaded by influences from the two superior adjacent cultures. One would expect the newcomers to have assimilated alien modes of thought, since these were supported by such vast prestige. Untold immigrants from deserts and mountains had done so in the past; and many individual Hebrews did, in fact, conform to the ways of the Gentiles. But assimilation was not characteristic for Hebrew thought. On the contrary, it held out with a peculiar stubbornness and insolence against the wisdom of Israel's neighbors. It is possible to detect the reflection of Egyptian and Mesopotamian beliefs in many episodes of the Old Testament; but the overwhelming impression left by that document is one, not of derivation, but of originality.

The dominant tenet of Hebrew thought is the absolute transcendence of God. Yahweh is not in nature. Neither earth nor sun nor heaven is divine; even the most potent natural phenomena are but reflections of God's greatness. It is not even possible properly to name God:

And Moses said unto God, Behold, when I come unto the children of Israel and shall say unto them, The God of your fathers hath sent me unto you; and they shall say to me: What is his name? what shall I say unto them?

And God said unto Moses: I AM THAT I AM: and he said, Thus shalt thou say unto the children of Israel, I AM hath sent me unto you (Exod. 3:13–14).

The God of the Hebrews is pure being, unqualified, ineffable. He is *holy*. That means that he is *sui generis*. It does not mean that he is taboo or that he is power. It means that all values are ultimately attributes of God alone. Hence, all concrete phenomena are devaluated. . . . In Hebrew thought man and nature are not necessarily corrupt; but both are necessarily *valueless* before God. As Eliphaz said to Job (and we use the Chicago translation):

Can a mortal be righteous before God
Or a man be pure before his Maker?
Even in his servants he does not trust,
And his angels he charges with error.
How much less them that dwell in houses of
   clay,
Whose foundation is in the dust. . . .
                              (Job 4:17–19*a*).

A similar meaning lies in the words of Deutero-Isaiah (64:6*a*): "We are all as an unclean thing, and all our righteousnesses are as filthy rags." Even man's righteousness, his highest virtue, is devaluated by the comparison with the absolute.

In the field of material culture such a conception of God leads to iconoclasm; and it needs an effort of the imagination to realize the shattering boldness of a contempt for imagery at the time, and in the particular historical setting, of the Hebrews. Everywhere religious fervor not only inspired verse and rite but also sought plastic and pictorial expression. The Hebrews, however, denied the relevancy of the "graven image"; the boundless could not be given form, the unqualified could but be offended by a representation, whatever the skill and the devotion that went into its making. Every finite reality shriveled to nothingness before the absolute value which was God.

The abysmal difference between the Hebrew and the normal Near Eastern viewpoints can best be illustrated by the manner in which an identical theme, the instability of the social order, is treated. We have a number of Egyptian texts which deal with the period of social upheaval which followed the great era of the pyramid builders. The disturbance of the established order was viewed with horror. Neferrohu said:

I show thee the land in lamentation and distress. The man with a weak arm (now) has (a strong) arm. . . . I show thee how the undermost is turned to uppermost. . . . The poor man will acquire riches.

The most famous of the sages, Ipuwer, is even more explicit. For instance, he condemns as a disastrous parody of order the fact that

gold and lapis lazuli are hung about the necks of slave girls. But noble ladies walk through the land and mistresses of houses say: Would that we had something to eat. . . . Behold they that possessed beds now lie upon the ground. He that slept with dirt upon him now stuffeth for himself a cushion.

The upshot is unmitigated misery for all: "Nay but great and small say: I wish I were dead."

In the Old Testament we meet the same theme — the reversal of established social conditions. When Hannah, after years of barrenness, had prayed for a son, and Samuel was born, she praised God:

There is none holy as the Lord: for there is none beside thee: neither is there any rock like our God. . . . The bows of the mighty men are broken, and they that stumbled are girded with strength. They that were full have hired out themselves for bread; and they that were hungry ceased. . . . The Lord maketh poor and maketh rich: he bringeth low, and lifteth up. He raiseth up the poor out of the dust, and lifteth up the beggar from the dunghill, to set them among princes, and to make them inherit the throne of glory: for the pillars of the earth are the Lord's and he hath set the world upon them (I Sam. 2:2–8).

Notice that the last verses state explicitly that God created the existing social order; but, quite characteristically, this order did not derive any sacredness, any value, from its divine origin. The sacredness and value remain attributes of God alone, and the violent changes of fortune observed in social life are but signs of God's omnipotence. Nowhere else do we meet this fanatical devaluation of the phenomena of nature and the achievements of man: art, virtue, social order — in view of the unique significance of the divine. It has been rightly pointed out that the monotheism of the Hebrews is a correlate of their insistence on the unconditioned nature of God. Only a God who transcends every phenomenon, who is not conditioned by any mode of manifestation — only an unqualified God can be the one and only ground of *all* existence.

This conception of God represents so high a degree of abstraction that, in reaching it, the Hebrews seem to have left the realm of mythopoeic thought. The impression that they did so is strengthened when we observe that the Old Testament is remarkably poor in mythology of the type we have encountered in Egypt and Mesopotamia. But this impression requires correction. The processes of mythopoeic thought are decisive for many sections of the Old Testament. For instance, the magnificent verses from the Book of Proverbs . . . describe the Wisdom of God, personified and substantialized in the same manner in which the corresponding concept of *ma'at* is treated by the Egyptians. Even the great conception of an only and transcendent God was not entirely free from myth, for it was not the fruit of detached speculation but of a passionate and dynamic experi-

ence. Hebrew thought did not entirely overcome mythopoeic thought. It created, in fact, a new myth — the myth of the Will of God.

Although the great "Thou" which confronted the Hebrews transcended nature, it stood in a specific relationship to the people. For when they were freed from bondage and roamed in "a desert land . . . the waste howling wilderness . . . the Lord alone did lead (them) and there was no strange god with (them)" (Deut. 32:10–12). And God had said:

But thou, Israel, art my servant, Jacob whom I have chosen, the seed of Abraham my friend. Thou whom I have taken from the ends of the earth, and called thee from the chief men thereof, and said unto thee, Thou art my servant; I have chosen thee, and not cast thee away (Isa. 41:8–9).

Thus God's will was felt to be focused on one particular and concrete group of human beings; it was asserted to have manifested itself at one decisive moment in their history and ceaselessly and relentlessly to have urged, rewarded, or chastised the people of its choice. For in Sinai, God had said, "Ye shall be unto me a kingdom of priests and an holy nation" (Exod. 19:6).

It is a poignant myth, this Hebrew myth of a chosen people, of a divine promise made, of a terrifying moral burden imposed — a prelude to the later myth of the Kingdom of God, that more remote and more spiritual "promised land." For in the myth of the chosen people the ineffable majesty of God and the worthlessness of man are correlated in a dramatic situation that is to unfold in time and is moving toward a future where the distant yet related parallels of human and divine existence are to meet in infinity.

Not cosmic phenomena, but history itself, had here become pregnant with meaning; history had become a revelation of the dynamic will of God. The human being was not merely the servant of the god as he was in Mesopotamia; nor was he placed, as in Egypt, at a preordained station in a static universe which did not need to be — and, in fact, could not be — questioned. Man, according to Hebrew thought, was the interpreter and the servant of God; he was even honored with the task of bringing about the realization of God's will. Thus man was condemned to unending efforts which were doomed to fail because of his inadequacy. In the Old Testament we find man possessed of a new freedom and of a new burden of responsibility. We also find there a new and utter lack of *eudaimonia,* of harmony — whether with the world of reason or with the world of perception.

All this may help to explain the strange poignancy of single individuals in the Old Testament. Nowhere in the literature of Egypt or Babylonia do we meet the loneliness of the biblical figures, astonishingly real in their mixture of ugliness and beauty, pride and contrition, achievement and failure. There is the tragic figure of Saul, the problematical David; there are countless others. We find single men in terrible isolation facing a transcendent God: Abraham trudging to the place of sacrifice with his son, Jacob in his struggle, and Moses and the prophets. In Egypt and Mesopotamia man was dominated, but also supported, by the great rhythm of nature. If in his dark moments he felt himself caught and held in the net of unfathomable decisions, his involvement in nature had, on the whole, a soothing character. He was gently carried along on the perennial cosmic tides of the seasons. The depth and intimacy of man's relationship with nature found expression in the ancient symbol of the mother-goddess. But Hebrew thought ignored this image entirely. It only recognized the stern Father, of whom it was said: "he led him (Jacob, the people) about, he instructed him, he kept him as the apple of his eye" (Deut. 32:10*b*).

The bond between Yahweh and his chosen people had been finally established during the Exodus. The Hebrews considered the forty years in the desert the decisive phase in their development. And we, too, may understand the originality and the coherence of their speculations if we relate them to their experience in the desert.

Preceding chapters took great care to describe the Egyptian and Mesopotamian landscapes. In doing so, the authors did not succumb to an unwarranted naturalism; they did not claim that cultural phenomena could be derived from physiographical causes. They merely suggested that a relation between land and culture may exist, a suggestion we can accept the more readily since we have seen that the surrounding world confronted early man as a "Thou." We may ask, then, what was the natural setting which determined the Hebrew's experience of the world around him. Now, the Hebrews, whatever their ancestry and historical antecedents, were tribal nomads. And since they were nomads in the Near East, they must have lived, not in boundless steppes, but between the desert and the sown, between the most fertile of lands and the total negation of life, which, in this remarkable corner of the earth, lie cheek by jowl. They must, therefore, have known through experience both the reward and the cost of existence in either.

The Hebrews craved to settle for good in the fertile plains. But characteristically they dreamed of lands overflowing with milk and honey, not lands of superabundant crops like those the Egyptians imagined for their hereafter. It seems that the desert as a metaphysical experience loomed very large for the Hebrews and colored all their valuations. It is, perhaps, the tension between two valuations — between a desire and a contempt for what is desired — that may explain some of the paradoxes of ancient Hebrew beliefs.

The organized states of the ancient Near East were agricultural; but the values of an agricultural community are the opposites of those of the nomadic tribe, especially of the extreme type of nomads of the desert. The settled peasant's reverence for impersonal authority, and the bondage, the constraint which the organized state imposes, mean an intolerable lack of personal freedom for the tribesman. The farmer's everlasting preoccupation with phenomena of growth and his total dependence on these phenomena appear to the nomad a form of slavery. Moreover, to him the desert is clean, but the scene of life, which is also the scene of decay, is sordid.

On the other hand, nomadic freedom can be bought only at a price; for whoever rejects the complexities and mutual dependencies of agricultural society not only gains freedom but also loses the bond with the phenomenal world; in fact, he gains his freedom at the cost of significant form. For, wherever we find reverence for the phenomena of life and growth, we find preoccupation with the immanence of the divine and with the *form* of its manifestation. But in the stark solitude of the desert, where nothing changes, nothing moves (except man at his own free will), where features in the landscape are only pointers, landmarks, without significance in themselves — there we may expect the image of God to transcend concrete phenomena altogether. Man confronting God will not contemplate him but will hear his voice and command, as Moses did, and the prophets, and Mohammed.

When we compare the lands of origin of Hebrews, Egyptians, and Mesopotamians, we [are] concerned, not with the relation between group psychology and habitat, but with profound differences in pristine religious experience. The peculiar experience which we have just described seems characteristic for all the most significant figures of the Old Testament. It is important to realize this, not because it enables us to understand them better as individuals, but because we then recognize what colored and integrated their thought. They propounded, not speculative theory, but revolutionary and dynamic teaching. The doctrine of a single, unconditioned, transcendent God rejected time-honored values, proclaimed new ones, and postulated a metaphysical significance for history and for man's actions. With infinite *moral* courage the Hebrews worshiped an absolute God and accepted as the correlate of their faith the sacrifice of a harmonious existence. In transcending the Near Eastern myths of immanent godhead, they created, as we have seen, the new myth of the will of God. It remained for the Greeks, with their peculiar *intellectual* courage, to discover a form of speculative thought in which myth was entirely overcome.

Noah and Utnapishtim

ALEXANDER HEIDEL

Alexander Heidel, born in Argentina in 1907 and educated at Lutheran seminaries in Brazil and the United States, received his Ph.D. from the University of Chicago. In 1932 he became a research assistant to the Assyrian Dictionary Project at Chicago. Dr. Heidel died in 1955. The following selection compares the biblical flood story with its Mesopotamian analog, in which the Mesopotamian Noah, Utnapishtim, describes the flood to the hero Gilgamesh.

IN THE EVENING the leader of the sto[rm(?)] caused a destructive rain to rain down.
I viewed the appearance of the weather;
The weather was frightful to behold.
I entered the ship and closed my door.
For the navigation(?) of the ship to the boatman Puzur-Amurri
I intrusted the mighty structure with its goods.
As soon as the first shimmer of morning beamed forth,
A black cloud came up from out the horizon.
Adad thunders within it,
While Shullat and Ḥanish go before,
Coming as heralds over hill and plain;
Irragal pulls out the masts;
Ninurta comes along (and) causes the dikes to give way;
The Anunnaki raised (their) torches,
Lighting up the land with their brightness;
The raging of Adad reached unto heaven
(And) turned into darkness all that was light.
[. . .] the land he broke(?) like a po[t(?)].
(For) one day the tem[pest blew].
Fast it blew and [. . .].
Like a battle [it ca]me over the p[eople].
No man could see his fellow.
The people could not be recognized from heaven.

(Even) the gods were terror-stricken at the deluge.
They fled (and) ascended to the heaven of Anu;
The gods cowered like dogs (and) crouched in distress(?).
Ishtar cried out like a woman in travail;
The lovely-voiced Lady of the g[ods] lamented:
"In truth, the olden time has turned to clay,
Because I commanded evil in the assembly of the gods!
How could I command (such) evil in the assembly of the gods!
(How) could I command war to destroy my people,
(For) it is I who bring forth (these) my people!
Like the spawn of fish they (now) fill the sea!"
The Anunnaki-gods wept with her;
The gods sat bowed (and) weeping.
Covered were their lips . . .
Six days and [six] nights
The wind blew, the downpour, the tempest, (and) the flo[od] overwhelmed the land.
When the seventh day arrived, the tempest, the flood,
Which had fought like an army, subsided in (its) onslaught.
The sea grew quiet, the storm abated, the flood ceased.

Reprinted from *The Gilgamesh Epic and Old Testament Parallels* by Alexander Heidel, pp. 84–88, 224–230, 248–249, 268–269, by permission of The University of Chicago Press. Copyright 1946 and 1949 by The University of Chicago.

I opened a window, and light fell upon my face.

I looked upon the sea, (all) was silence,
And all mankind had turned to clay;
The . . . was as level as a (flat) roof.
I bowed, sat down, and wept,
My tears running down over my face.
I looked in (all) directions for the boundaries of the sea.
At (a distance of) twelve (double-hours) there emerged a stretch of land.
On Mount Niṣir the ship landed.
Mount Niṣir held the ship fast and did not let (it) move.
One day, a second day Mount Niṣir held the ship fast and did not let (it) move.
A third day, a fourth day Mount Niṣir held the ship fast and did not let (it) move.
A fifth day, a sixth day Mount Niṣir held the ship fast and did not let (it) move.
When the seventh day arrived,
I sent forth a dove and let (her) go.
The dove went away and came back to me;
There was no resting-place, and so she returned.
(Then) I sent forth a swallow and let (her) go.
The swallow went away and came back to me;
There was no resting-place, and so she returned.
(Then) I sent forth a raven and let (her) go.
The raven went away, and when she saw that the waters had abated,
She ate, she flew about, she cawed, (and) did not return.
(Then) I sent forth (everything) to the four winds and offered a sacrifice.
I poured out a libation on the peak of the mountain.
Seven and (yet) seven kettles I set up.
Under them I heaped up (sweet) cane, cedar, and myrtle.
The gods smelled the savor,
The gods smelled the sweet savor.
The gods gathered like flies over the sacrificer.
As soon as the great goddess arrived,
She lifted up the great jewels which Anu had made according to her wish:

"O ye gods here present, as surely as I shall not forget the lapis lazuli on my neck,
I shall remember these days and shall not forget (them) ever!
Let the gods come near to the offering;
(But) Enlil shall not come near to the offering,
Because without reflection he brought on the deluge
And consigned my people to destruction!"
As soon as Enlil arrived
And saw the ship, Enlil was wroth;
He was filled with anger against the gods, the Igigi:
"Has any of the mortals escaped? No man was to live through the destruction!"
Ninurta opened his mouth and said, speaking to warrior Enl[il]:
"Who can do things without Ea?
For Ea alone understands every matter."
Ea opened his mouth and said, speaking to warrior Enlil:
"O warrior, thou wisest among the gods!
How, O how couldst thou without reflection bring on (this) deluge?
On the sinner lay his sin; on the transgressor lay his transgression!
Let loose, that he shall not be cut off; pull tight, that he may not ge[t (too) loose]
Instead of thy sending a deluge, would that a lion had come and diminished mankind!
(Or) instead of thy sending a deluge, would that a wolf had come and dim[inished] mankind!
(Or) instead of thy sending a deluge, would that a famine had occurred and [destroyed] the land!
(Or) instead of thy sending a deluge, would that Irra had come and smitten mankind!
(Moreover,) it was not I who revealed the secret of the great gods;
(But) to Atraḫasis I showed a dream, and so he learned the secret of the gods.
And now take counsel concerning him."
Then Enlil went up into the ship.
He took my hand and caused me to go aboard.

He caused my wife to go aboard (and) to
kneel down at my side.
Standing between us, he touched our fore-
heads and blessed us:
"Hitherto Utnapishtim has been but a man;
But now Utnapishtim and his wife shall be
like unto us gods.
In the distance, at the mouth of the rivers,
Utnapishtim shall dwell!"
So they took me and caused me to dwell in
the distance, at the mouth of the rivers.

* * *

The most remarkable parallels between
the Old Testament and the Gilgamesh Epic
— in fact, the most remarkable parallels between the Old Testament and the entire
corpus of cuneiform inscriptions from Mesopotamia — are found in the deluge accounts
of the Babylonians and Assyrians, on the
one hand, and the Hebrews, on the other.
With the study of this material we therefore
enter a field which, a priori, should prove
most fruitful in our examination of the
genetic relationship between the Mesopotamian records and our Old Testament
literature. Here, if anywhere, we should
expect to find evidence enabling us to decide the question whether any part of the
Old Testament has been derived from
Babylonian sources. It is therefore with
special interest that we shall make the following inquiry.

The Book of Genesis, consonant with
Hebrew monotheism, attributes the sending
of the deluge to the one and only true God
recognized in the Old Testament, while
the cuneiform tablets represent a multitude
of divinities as engaged in bringing about
this fearful catastrophe. . . .

As the cause for the cataclysm, the Old
Testament emphasizes the moral depravity
of the human race. Man could have averted
this unparalleled destruction of life if he
had conformed his ways to the will of his
Maker, but instead of that he followed his
own inclinations. The whole bent of the

thoughts of his heart was never anything
but evil. The earth was corrupt before God
and was filled with violence because of
man, for all flesh had corrupted its way
upon the earth (Gen. 6:1–13).

In the Gilgamesh Epic the reason for the
deluge is not nearly so apparent as it is in
the Book of Genesis. The opening lines of
the flood story contained in the epic state
simply that the heart of the great gods
prompted them to bring a deluge. From
this passage one might get the impression
that the flood was due to divine caprice.
But according to Ea's speech toward the
close of the account, where he reprimands
Enlil for this thoughtless and unjustifiable
destruction, the flood was sent because of
the sin of man. Unfortunately, this does
not give us any clue as to the nature of
man's offense.

An answer to this question is given in
the fragmentary Atrahasis Epic. Starting
out much like Genesis, chapter 6, the epic
states that, when the people had multiplied
and, apparently, had become prosperous,
they became so noisy as to deprive Enlil of
his sleep. In an attempt to quiet them, Enlil
sent plague after plague. But, in the final
analysis, it was all of no avail; mankind
became more numerous (and evidently
more noisy) than before. In utter exaspera-
tion, Enlil at last sent the flood to destroy
them all and to put an end to their un-
bearable noise. . . .

In the Book of Genesis the deluge is a
righteous retribution for the sins of the un-
godly, while pious Noah and his family
are spared, with the full knowledge and the
express purpose of Him who sent the
flood. . . . But in the cuneiform inscriptions
the destruction is intended for all alike, for
the just as well as for the unjust, without
any exception whatsoever. This is particularly clear from the words with which Ea
reproached Enlil: "On the sinner 'lay his
sin; on the transgressor lay his transgression!" This line from the epic shows unmistakably that not *all* were sinners. Yet
had it not been for Ea's intervention, Enlil,
in his rashness, would have destroyed all

human and animal life without discrimination and thus would have defeated the very purpose for which, according to the Babylonian creation stories, mankind and the animals had been created, viz., to supply the wants of the gods. . . .

The manner in which the impending cataclysm was announced to the deluge hero in the Babylonian stories differs widely from the way in which it was revealed to the Old Testament Noah. . . . [In the Gilgamesh Epic] this warning took place while Utnapishtim lay asleep in the reed hut, for, when Ea was taken to account by Enlil for having divulged the secret of the gods, he tried to justify his course of action by asserting that it really was not he who had revealed the divine resolution but that he had shown a dream to Utnapishtim and that from this dream "the exceedingly wise" had guessed the plan of the great gods. . . . Utnapishtim was not told expressly, in the Gilgamesh Epic, that a deluge would be sent in which all mankind was to perish, but he was told enough so that he could draw the necessary conclusions. This revelation was made not only without the knowledge of Enlil, the real author of the flood, but it was also quite contrary to his plan, according to which "no man was to live through the destruction."

In Genesis, on the other hand, Noah apparently received a direct communication; there is no indication that the will of God was conveyed to him through the medium of a dream. Furthermore, the disclosure was made by the Lord himself, and was therefore in full accord with his purpose. The God who caused the flood also saved his faithful servant by informing him of the approaching catastrophe and by ordering the building of an ark. However, all available accounts agree that the impending peril was divinely announced to the hero of the deluge.

According to Gen. 6:3, man was granted a period of grace extending over one hundred and twenty years, during which he had an opportunity to amend his sinful ways and to avert the threatened destruction. . . .

In the Gilgamesh Epic there was no thought of granting mankind an opportunity to repent. There the planned destruction of the human race was a zealously guarded secret of the gods. It was such an inviolable secret that even as great a divinity as Ea did not dare to communicate it directly to his favorite, Utnapishtim, but felt compelled to resort to a subterfuge, by warning the latter in a dream from which he could guess the contents of the gods' decree. . . .

The magnitude of the storm and its appalling effect are described in forceful terms in the main Babylonian recension of the deluge. . . . The tempest raged in all its fury and apparently assumed greater dimensions than many of the gods had anticipated, for, terror-stricken at the frightful cataclysm, they fled to the highest heaven and cowered like dogs in their distress! Ishtar, the lovely voiced lady of the gods, cried out like a woman in travail and lamented: "In truth, the olden time has turned to clay, because I commanded evil in the assembly of the gods! How could I command (such) evil in the assembly of the gods! (How) could I command war to destroy my people, (for) it is I who bring forth (these) my people! Like the spawn of fish they (now) fill the sea!" Even the Anunnaki, who had helped to spread terror and destruction among mankind, wept with her. "The gods sat bowed (and) weeping. Covered were their lips.". . .

As in the case of the creation stories, we still do not know how the biblical and Babylonian narratives of the deluge are related historically. The available evidence proves nothing beyond the point that there is a genetic relationship between Genesis and the Babylonian versions. The skeleton is the same in both cases, but the flesh and blood and, above all, the animating spirit are different. It is here that we meet the most far-reaching divergencies between the Hebrew and the Mesopotamian stories.

The main Babylonian flood legend, in particular, is "steeped in the silliest polytheism," to quote the words of Dillmann. The gods are divided in their counsel, false to one another and to man; they flee in consternation to the highest heaven and cower like dogs in their distress; they quarrel and lie and gather over the sacrificer like a swarm of hungry flies! In the Babylonian accounts the moral or ethical motive is almost completely absent. As we read the first few lines of the flood story on Tablet XI of the Gilgamesh Epic, we get the impression that the cataclysm was caused by the caprice of the gods, for no ethical reason at all; however, toward the end of the story we are told, quite incidentally and by implication only, that the flood was due to the sin of mankind. Wherein the sin consisted is not indicated. According to the Atrahasis Epic, the flood was sent because mankind with their noisy, hilarious gatherings disturbed the sleep of Enlil. Some such idea may also have been in the minds of the authors of the flood tradition in the Gilgamesh Epic. In none of the other Babylonian legends do we find any reason at all for the deluge, an omission which may, however, be due solely to the imperfect state in which they have come down to us. At any rate, in the Babylonian stories it is nowhere emphasized that the gods were actuated by moral ideals or that the flood was a divine visitation on human corruption. Rather, considering that the gods were intent on destroying the whole human race without discrimination between the just and the unjust, it is apparent that the gods were prompted more by caprice than by a sense of justice. It is true, the deluge hero was saved by a friendly deity because of his piety; but that was done clandestinely, through trickery, and against the decree of the gods in council.

In the biblical story, on the other hand, the flood is sent by the one omnipotent God, who is just in all his dealings with the children of men, who punishes the impenitent sinner, even if it means the destruction of the world, but who saves the just with his powerful hand and in his own way. In Genesis the deluge is clearly and unmistakably a moral judgment, a forceful illustration of divine justice meting out stern punishment to a "faithless and perverse generation" but delivering the righteous. What a serious view the biblical account takes of the moral depravity of the prediluvian race of men can be seen also ... from the fact that in it no tears are shed ... over those who perished in the flood; theirs was a just and deserved punishment. In the Hebrew document the ethical motive is so strong that God is portrayed even as regretting the very creation of man; while in the Babylonian, the gods, with the possible exception of Enlil, regret the destruction of man. Although God resolves not to send another flood, he is nowhere represented as *regretting* the diluvial catastrophe. Irrespective of whether or not the Hebrew account is to some degree dependent on Babylonian material also, this piece of biblical literature was "written for our learning" (Rom. 15:4), in order to rouse the conscience of the world and to give hope and comfort to the God-fearing.

The Ethical Implications of Monotheism

STEWART C. EASTON

Stewart C. Easton was born in Cheshire, England in 1907. After obtaining degrees from universities in Canada and the United States, Dr. Easton taught history at the City College of New York from 1947 to 1960. He now devotes most of his time to writing.

THE HEBREWS are, of course, credited above all with the formulation of monotheism, the worship of one God; and this monotheism has been transmitted both to Christianity and to Islam, so that it is the fundamental religious belief of the West. But it is not always recognized that they are also responsible for the precise definition of the nature of sin; and their thought upon the question of sin and punishment has permeated Western thought as deeply as has the concept of monotheism itself. . . .

IMPORTANCE OF MONOTHEISM FOR MORALITY

The supreme consequence of the Hebrew concept is in the field of human morality. Because God is a person, he can take part in human affairs, guiding them, rewarding and punishing his children, thus upholding the moral order. This monotheism is clearly an advance on Mesopotamian thought, since the many gods of the Babylonians were conceived of as so many arbitrary but powerful beings competing for man's worship. Each man had a personal god who was expected to use his influence with the higher gods on behalf of his protégé, as human beings use political influence to ensure personal favors. And among the higher gods it was impossible for a man to choose which to petition. He could not tell which one he had offended, nor did he know what was demanded of him.

Polytheism cannot escape the dilemma that the different gods may issue contradictory demands; unless these gods may be said to have agreed among themselves on what to demand from man, their different commands will necessarily at some time conflict with each other. The separate gods can only reward and punish in accordance with their limited power, and thus cannot command obedience from man and insist upon it on pain of punishment. Shamash, the Babylonian god of the sun and of justice, might give Hammurabi a code of laws, but it was only by virtue of his function as lawgiver among the numerous Babylonian gods. The Babylonian did not regard him as the enforcer of the laws, nor did he pray to Shamash to mitigate his severity. This was the task of the personal god of the Babylonian, who used his influence among his superiors in the pantheon.

But the Hebrew God, being one, not a force of nature but a transcendent being, separate from the world yet immanent in it, could act as ruler and governor, first of his chosen people and then of the whole world. He could issue a law which instructed the people as to exactly what he expected of them, could define disobedience to the law as sin, and could take steps to see that he was obeyed. The law thus removed any doubt in the sinner's mind as to what he was expected to do, and what was forbidden him, and held out the hope that if he fulfilled these duties toward God he would be prosperous and happy. . . . The following quotations from Babylonian and Hebrew documents will serve to point the contrast between the two attitudes, and reveal at the same time how greatly the Hebrew felt he had been privileged when God gave him his Law.

The Babylonian: "What is good in one's sight is evil for a god, what is bad in one's own mind is good for his god. Who can understand the counsel of the gods in the midst of heaven? Where has befuddled mankind ever learned what a god's conduct is?" Again: "Man is dumb; he knows nothing. Mankind, everyone that exists — what does he know? Whether he is committing sin or doing good he does not even know."

The Hebrew: "I have stored thy message in my heart that I may not sin against thee. . . . With my lips I recount all the ordinances of thy mouth. In the way of thy decrees I delight, as much as in all wealth. I meditate upon thy precepts, and I observe thy paths. I find joy in thy statutes, I will not forget thy word. . . At midnight I rise up to give thee thanks because of thy righteous ordinances . . . the law of thy mouth is worth more to me than thousands in gold and silver."

Hebrew monotheism, then, with its consequent belief that God rewarded and punished men in accordance with their deeds, has been of incalculable importance in the religious and psychological history of mankind.

III. THE EGYPTIAN QUESTION

Akhnaton, The First Monotheist

JAMES HENRY BREASTED

James Henry Breasted was born in Rockford, Illinois in 1865. He was educated at Yale and at the University of Berlin, where he received a Ph.D. in 1894. His dissertation dealt with the hymns of Akhnaton. Breasted joined the faculty of the University of Chicago in 1895 as the first teacher of Egyptology in America. In 1919 he founded Chicago University's Oriental Institute. He retired in 1933 and died two years later. His works include *A History of Egypt* and *Development of Religion and Thought in Ancient Egypt*.

IN THE FEUDAL AGE the *social* realm had made its deepest impression upon religion and morals as in the Pyramid Age the Egyptian state, the *political* realm, had earlier done. Both of these were limited to the territory of Egypt. To be sure, the Pyramid Age had gained a dim vision of the vast extent of the Sun-god's [Re's] dominion, and in the Pyramid Texts he is once addressed by the sounding title, "Limitless.". . . The Pyramid Age, in the social discernment of such men as Ptahhotep, had created a realm of universal ethical values, and in giving the Sun-god the sovereignty of such a realm the Egyptians were already moving on the road towards monotheism. We recall that the instruction of the unknown Heracleopolitan king had likewise carried the Egyptians a long way on that road. Through the conception of a great administrative and moral order, for which they had already developed a word, the Egyptians might have advanced to full recognition of monotheism as later philosophers and theologians have done. Nevertheless, in the Pyramid Age this moral order had remained a *national* conception and it was not extended to embrace the world as a whole.

The Sun-god ruled only Egypt, and in the great sun-hymn of the Pyramid Texts he stands guardian on the Egyptian frontiers, where he builds the gates which restrain all outsiders from entering his inviolable domain. In the Pyramid Age, too, the Sun-god had already begun the process of absorbing the other gods of Egypt, a process resulting even at so remote a date in a form of national pantheism, in which all the gods ultimately coalesced into forms and functions of one. But even this process, though it did not cease, had left the supreme god's dominion still restricted to Egypt. He was very far from being a world-god. The Egyptians indeed had not as yet gained the world-idea, the world-empire over which they might install the world-ruler. The influences of an environment restricted to the limits of the Nile Valley had now, however, gone as far as they could, when a career of imposing foreign expansion of national power enlarged the theatre of thought and action. The Solar theology had been sensitively responsive to conditions in the Nile-Valley world. It proved to be not less sensitive to the larger world, to include which the Egyptian horizon had now expanded.

Egypt's imperial expansion northward and southward until the Pharaoh's power had united the contiguous regions of Asia and Africa into the first stable Empire in history is the commanding fact in the history of the East in the sixteenth century B.C. The consolidation of that power by Thutmose III's twenty years' campaigning in Asia is a stirring chapter of military imperialism in which for the first time in the East we can discern the skilfully organized and mobile forces of a great state as they are brought to bear with incessant impact upon the nations of Western Asia, until the Egyptian supremacy is undisputed from the Greek Islands, the coasts of Asia Minor, and the highlands of the Upper Euphrates on the north to the Fourth Cataract of the Nile on the south. This great military leader himself made the remark which we have quoted above regarding his god: "He seeth the whole earth hourly." If this was true it was because the sword of the Pharaoh had carried the power of Egypt's god to the limit of Egypt's Empire. Fifty years earlier, indeed, Thutmose I proclaimed his kingdom as far as "the circuit of the sun." In the Old Kingdom the Sun-god was conceived as a Pharaoh whose kingdom was Egypt. With the expansion of the Egyptian kingdom into a world-empire it was inevitable that the domain of the god should likewise expand. As the kingdom had long since found expression in religion, so now the Empire was to make a powerful impression upon religious thought.

While this was a more or less mechanical and unconscious process, it was accompanied by an intellectual awakening which shook the old Egyptian traditions to the foundations and set the men of the age to thinking in a larger world. The Sun-god had been an Egyptian Pharaoh for two thousand five hundred years, a Pharaoh ruling Egypt; but after 1600 B.C. the Pharaoh became lord of the civilized world. The conqueror Thutmose III was the first character of universal aspects in human history, the first world-hero. As such he made a profound impression upon his age. The idea of universal power, of a world-empire, was visibly and tangibly bodied forth in his career. There is a touch of universalism now discernible in the theology of the Empire which is directly due to such impressions as he and his successors made. Egypt is forced out of the immemorial isolation of her narrow valley into world-relations, with which the theology of the time must reckon — relations with which the Sun-god, as we have seen, was inextricably involved. Commercial connections, maintained from an immemorially remote past, had not sufficed to bring the great outside world effectively into the purview of Egyptian thinking. The limits of the dominion of the Egyptian gods had been fixed as the outer fringes of the Nile Valley long before the outside world was familiar to the Nile-dwellers; and merely commercial intercourse with a larger world had not been able to shake the tradition. Many a merchant had seen a stone fall in distant Babylon and in Egyptian Thebes alike, but it had not occurred to him, or to any man in that far-off age, that the same natural force pulling down the falling stone reigned in both these widely separated countries. The world was far indeed from the lad lying beneath the apple-tree and discovering a universal force in the fall of an apple. Many a merchant of that day, too, had seen the sun rise behind the Babylonian tower-temples as it did among the clustered obelisks of Thebes, but the thought of the age had not yet come to terms with such far-reaching facts as these, even though the Conqueror himself had said of the Sun-god, "He seeth the whole earth hourly." It was universalism expressed in terms of imperial power which first caught the imagination of the thinking men of the Empire, and disclosed to them the universal sweep of the

Sun-god's dominion as a physical fact. Monotheism was but imperialism in religion.

It is no accident, therefore, that about 1400 B.C., in the reign of Amenhotep III, the most splendid of the Egyptian emperors, we find the first of such impressions. Two architects, Suti and Hor, twin brothers, whom Amenhotep III was employing at Thebes, have left us a sun-hymn on a stela now in the British Museum, which discloses the tendency of the age and the widening vision with which these men of the Empire were looking out upon the world and discerning the unlimited scope of the Sun-god's realm. This sun-hymn contains such significant lines as these:

Thou art a craftsman shaping thine own limbs;
Fashioner without being fashioned;
Unique in his qualities, traversing eternity;
Over ways with millions under his guidance. . . .

When thou sailest across the sky all men behold thee,
(Though) thy going is hidden from their sight. . . .

Thou traversest a journey of leagues,
Even millions and hundred-thousands of time.
Every day is under thee.
When thy setting comes,
The hours of the night hearken to thee likewise.
When thou hast traversed it
There comes no ending to thy labours.
All men, they see by means of thee. . . .

Creator of all and giver of their sustenance, . . .

A mother, profitable to gods and men,
A craftsman of experience, . . .
Valiant herdman who drives his cattle,
Their refuge and giver of their sustenance, . . .

Who beholds that which he has made,
Sole lord taking captive all lands every day,

As one beholding them that walk therein;
Shining in the sky, a being as the sun.
He makes the seasons by the months,
Heat when he desires,
Cold when he desires, . . .

Every land is in rejoicing
At his rising every day, in order to praise him.

It is evident in such a hymn as this that the vast sweep of the Sun-god's course over all the lands and peoples of the earth has at last found consideration, . . . and the momentous step has been taken of extending the sway of the Sun-god over all lands and peoples. No earlier document left us by the thought of Egypt contains such unequivocal expression of this thought as we find here:

Sole lord, taking captive all lands every day,
As one beholding them that walk therein.

It is important to observe also that this tendency is connected directly with the social movement of the Feudal Age. Such epithets applied to the Sun-god as

Valiant herdman who drives his cattle,
Their refuge and the giver of their sustenance,

of course carry us back to the Instruction Addressed to Merikere, in which men are called "the flocks of God," and the thoughts of Ipuwer and his "shepherd of all men." The other remarkable epithet,

A mother, profitable to gods and men,

carries with it the idea of similar solicitude for mankind. The humane aspects of the Sun-god's sway, to which the social thinkers of the Feudal Age chiefly contributed, have not disappeared among the powerful political motives of this new universalism.

When Amenhotep III's son, Amenhotep IV, succeeded his father, about 1375 B.C., a keen struggle arose between the royal house, on the one hand, and the sacerdotal organization dominated by Amon, on the other. It is evident that the young king favored the claims of the old Sun-god as opposed to those of Amon, whose powerful Theban priesthood had begun calling their once obscure local god by a composite name "Amon-Re," thus indicating his identity with the Sun-god Re. Early in his reign we find Amenhotep IV ardently supporting a new form of the old Solar faith, which may have been the result of a compromise between the two. At a time when the Asiatic situation was exceedingly critical, and the Pharaoh's supremacy there was threatened, he devoted himself with absorbing zeal to the new Solar universalism which we have discerned under his father. The Sun-god was given a designation which freed the new faith from the compromising polytheistic tradition of the old Solar theology. He was now called "Aton," an ancient name for the physical sun, and probably designating his disk. It occurs twice in the hymn of the two architects of Amenhotep III, quoted above, and it had already gained some favor under this king, who named one of his royal barges "Aton-Gleams." Not only did the Sun-god receive a new name, but the young king now gave him a new symbol also. We recall that the most ancient symbol of the Sun-god was a pyramid, and as a falcon the figure of that bird was also used to designate him. These, however, were intelligible only in Egypt, and Amenhotep IV had a wider arena in view. The new symbol depicted the sun as a disk from which diverging beams radiated downward, each ray terminating in a human hand. . . . It was a masterly symbol, suggesting a power issuing from its celestial source, and putting its hand upon the world and the affairs of men. As far back as the Pyramid Texts the rays of the Sun-god had been likened to his arms and had been conceived as an agency on earth: "The *arm* of the sunbeams is lifted with King Unis," raising him to the skies. Such a symbol was suited to be understood throughout the world which the Pharaoh controlled. Its meaning was so clear that an Asiatic on the Euphrates or a Nubian on the Sudanese Nile would discern its

significance at once. It was not only a symbol of universalism, but was supremely fitted to be a universal symbol.

There was also some effort to define the Solar power thus symbolized. The full name of the Sun-god was "Harakhte [Horizon-Horus], rejoicing in the horizon in his name 'Heat which is in Aton.'" It was enclosed in two royal cartouches, like the double name of the Pharaoh, a device suggested by the analogy of the Pharaoh's power, and another clear evidence of the impression which the Empire as a state had now made on the Solar theology. But the name enclosed in the cartouches roughly defined the actual physical force of the sun in the visible world, and was no political figure. The word rendered "heat" sometimes means also "light." It is evident that what the king was deifying was the force by which the Sun made himself felt on earth. In harmony with this conclusion are the numerous statements in the Aton hymns, which, as we shall see, represent Aton as everywhere active on earth by means of his "rays." While it is evident that the new faith drew its inspiration from Heliopolis, so that the king assuming the office of High Priest of Aton called himself "Great Seer," the title of the High Priest of Heliopolis, nevertheless most of the old lumber which made up the externals of the traditional theology was rejected. We look in vain for the sun-barques, and in the same way also later accretions, like the voyage through the subterranean caverns of the dead, are completely shorn away.

If the Aton movement was intended as a compromise with the priests of Amon, it failed. The bitterest enmities soon broke out, culminating finally in the determination on the king's part to make Aton sole god of the Empire and to annihilate Amon. The effort to obliterate all trace of the existence of the upstart Amon resulted in the most extreme measures. The king changed his own name from "Amenhotep" ("Amen rests" or "is satisfied") to "Ikhnaton," which means "Aton is satisfied," and is a translation of the king's old name into a corresponding idea in the Aton faith. The name of Amon, wherever it occurred on the great monuments of Thebes, was expunged, and in doing so not even the name of the king's father, Amenhotep III, was respected. These erasures were not confined to the name of Amon. Even the word "gods" as a compromising plural was expunged wherever found, and the names of the other gods, too, were treated like that of Amon.

Finding Thebes embarrassed with too many theological traditions, in spite of its prestige and its splendor, Ikhnaton forsook it and built a new capital about midway between Thebes and the sea, at a place now commonly known as Tell el-Amarna. He called it Akhetaton, "Horizon of Aton." A similar Aton city was founded in Nubia, and in all likelihood there was another in Asia. The three great portions of the Empire, Egypt, Nubia, and Syria, were thus each given a center of the Aton faith. Besides these, sanctuaries of Aton were also built at various other places in Egypt.

This was, of course, not accomplished without building up a powerful court party, which the king could oppose to the evicted priesthoods, especially that of Amon. The resulting convulsion undoubtedly affected seriously the power of the royal house. The life of this court party, which now unfolded at Akhetaton, centered about the propagation of the new faith, and as preserved to us in the wall reliefs which fill the chapels of the cliff tombs, excavated by the king for his nobles in the face of the low cliffs of the eastern plateau behind the new city, it forms, perhaps, the most interesting and picturesque chapter in the story of the early East. It is to the tombs of these partisans of the king that we owe our knowledge of the content of the remarkable teaching which he was now propagating. They contain a series of hymns in praise of the Sun-god, or of the Sun-god and the king alternately, which afford us at least a glimpse into the new world of thought, in which we behold this young king and his associates lifting up their eyes and endeavouring to discern God in the illimitable sweep of his power — God no longer of the Nile Valley only, but of all men and of all the world. We can do no better at this juncture than to let these hymns speak for themselves. The longest and most important is as follows:

UNIVERSAL SPLENDOUR AND POWER OF ATON

Thou dawnest beautifully in the horizon of the sky,
O living Aton who wast the Beginning of life!
When thou didst rise in the eastern horizon,
Thou didst fill every land with thy beauty.
Thou art beautiful, great, glittering, high over every land,
Thy rays, they encompass the lands, even to the end of all that thou hast made.
Thou art Re, and thou penetratest to the very end of them;
Thou bindest them for thy beloved son (the Pharaoh).
Though thou art far away; thy rays are upon earth;
Though thou art in the faces of men, thy footsteps are unseen.

NIGHT AND MAN

When thou settest in the western horizon of the sky,
The earth is in darkness like death.
They sleep in their chambers,
Their heads are wrapped up,
Their nostrils are stopped,
And none seeth the other,
While all their things are stolen,
Which are under their heads,
And they know it not.

Thou makest darkness, and it is night,
Wherein all the beasts of the forests creep
forth. (*Psalm* 104:20.)

NIGHT AND ANIMALS

Every lion cometh forth from his den,
All serpents, they sting.
Darkness broods,
The world is in silence,
He that made them resteth in his horizon.

The young lions roar after their prey,
And seek their food from God.
(*Psalm* 104:21.)

DAY AND MAN

Bright is the earth when thou risest in the
  horizon;
When thou shinest as Aton by day
Thou drivest away the darkness.
When thou sendest forth thy rays,
The Two Lands (Egypt) are in daily festivity.
Men waken and stand upon their feet
When thou hast raised them up.
Their limbs bathed, they take their clothing,
Their arms uplifted in adoration to thy
  dawning.
Then in all the world they do their work.

The sun ariseth, they get them away,
And lay them down in their dens.
Man goeth forth unto his work
And to his labour until the evening.
(*Psalm* 14:22–23.)

* * *

UNIVERSAL DOMINION

Thou didst make the distant sky in order to rise therein,
In order to behold all that thou hast made,
While thou wast yet alone
Shining in thy form as living Aton,
Dawning, glittering, going afar and returning.
Thou makest millions of forms
Through thyself alone;
Cities, villages, and fields, highways and rivers.
All eyes see thee before them,
For thou art Aton of the day over the earth.
When thou hast gone away,
And all men, whose faces thou hast fashioned
In order that thou mightest no longer see thyself alone,
[Have fallen asleep, so that not] one [seeth] that which thou hast made,
Yet art thou still in my heart.

REVELATION TO THE KING

. . . There is no other that knoweth thee
Save thy son Ikhnaton.
Thou hast made him wise
In thy designs and in thy might.

UNIVERSAL MAINTENANCE

The world subsists in thy hand,
Even as thou hast made them.
When thou hast risen they live,
When thou settest they die;
For thou art length of life of thyself,
Men live through thee.

The eyes of men see beauty
Until thou settest.

All labour is put away
When thou settest in the west.
When thou risest again
[Thou] makest [every hand] to flourish for the king
And [prosperity] is in every foot,
Since thou didst establish the world,
And raise them up for thy son,
Who came forth from thy flesh,
The king of Upper and Lower Egypt,
Living in Truth, Lord of the Two Lands,
Nefer-khepru-Re, Wan-Re (Ikhnaton),
Son of Re, living in Truth, lord of diadems,
Ikhnaton, whose life is long;
(And for) the chief royal wife, his beloved,
Mistress of the Two Lands, Nefer-nefru-Aton, Nofretete,
Living and flourishing for ever and ever.

* * *

In these hymns there is an inspiring universalism not found before, either in the thought of Egypt or in that of any other country. It is world-wide in its sweep. The king claims that the recognition of the Sun-god's universal supremacy is also universal, and that all men acknowledge his dominion. On the great boundary stela likewise he says of them, that Aton made them "for his own self; all lands, the Aegeans bear their dues, their tribute is upon their backs, for him who made their life, him by whose rays men live and breathe the air." It is clear that Ikhnaton was projecting a world religion, and endeavoring to displace by it the nationalism which had preceded it for twenty centuries.

Along with this universal power, Ikhnaton is also deeply impressed with the eternal duration of his god; and although he himself calmly accepts his own mortality, and early in his career at Amarna makes public and permanently records on the boundary stelae instructions for his own burial, nevertheless he relies upon his intimate relation with Aton to insure him something of the Sun-god's duration. His official titulary always contains the epithet after his name, "whose lifetime is long."

But in the beginning of all, Aton called himself forth out of the eternal solitude, the author of his own being. On one of the great boundary stelae at Amarna the king calls him "My rampart of a million cubits, my reminder of eternity, my witness of the things of eternity, who himself fashioned himself with his own hands, whom no artificer knew." In harmony with this idea, the hymns love to reiterate the fact that the creation of the world which followed was done while the god was yet alone. The words "while thou wert alone" are almost a refrain in these hymns. He is the universal creator who brought forth all the races of men and distinguished them in speech and color of skin. His creative power still goes on calling forth life, even from the inanimate egg. Nowhere do we find more marked the naïve wonder of the king at the Sun-god's life-giving power than in this marvel, that within the egg-shell, which the king calls the "stone" of the egg — within this lifeless stone, the sounds of life respond to the command of Aton, and, nourished by the breath which he gives, a living creature issues forth.

This life-giving power is the constant source of life and sustenance, and its immediate agency is the rays of the Sun, bringing light and heat to men. This extraordinary recognition of the Sun's energy as the source of all earthly life is constantly reiterated. The hymns love to dwell upon his rays as an ever-present universal power. "Thou art in the sky, but thy rays are on earth"; "Though thou art far away, thy rays are on earth"; "Thy rays are in the midst of the great green sea"; "Thy rays are on thy beloved son"; "He who makes whole the eyes by his rays"; "It is the breath of life in the nostrils to behold thy rays"; "Thy child (the king), who came forth from thy rays"; "Thou didst fashion him (the king) out of thine own rays"; "Thy rays carry a million royal jubilees"; "When thou sendest forth thy rays, the Two Lands are in festivity"; "Thy rays embrace the lands, even all that thou hast made"; "Whether he is in the sky or on earth, all eyes behold him without ceasing; he fills [every land] with his rays, and makes all men to live."

The obvious dependence of Egypt upon the Nile also made it impossible to ignore this source of life, and there is nothing which discloses more clearly the surprising rationalism of Ikhnaton than the fact that without hesitation he strips off the venerable body of myth and tradition which had for ages deified the Nile as Osiris, and thereupon attributes the inundation to natural forces controlled by his god, who in like solicitude for other lands has made a Nile for them in the sky. *Osiris is completely ignored.* He is never mentioned in any record of Ikhnaton or in any of the tombs at Amarna.

It is at this point that Ikhnaton's thought passes beyond a purely materialistic recognition of the Sun's activity on earth, and discerns the fatherly solicitude of Aton for all creatures. It is this thought which lifts the movement of Ikhnaton far above all that had before been attained in the religion of Egypt or of the whole East before this time. To Ipuwer the Sun-god was a kindly shepherd, and to Merikere's royal father men were his "flocks" for which he made air and water and food; but Ikhnaton goes further, and says to the Sun-god: "Thou art the father and the mother of all that thou hast made." This teaching is one which anticipates much of the later development in religion even down to our own time. To the sensitive soul of this Egyptian dreamer, the whole animate world seems alive with consciousness of

the presence of Aton, and filled with recognition of his fatherly kindness. The picture of the lily-grown marshes, where the flowers are "drunken" in the intoxicating radiance of Aton, where the birds unfold their wings and lift them "in adoration of the living Aton," where the cattle dance with delight in the sunshine, and the fish in the river beyond leap up to greet the light, the universal light whose beams are even "in the midst of the great green sea" — all this discloses a discernment of the universal presence of God in nature, and a mystic conviction of the recognition of that presence by all creatures. There is here an appreciation of the revelation of God in the visible world such as we find seven or eight hundred years later in the Hebrew psalms, and in our own poets of nature since Wordsworth.

It is evident that, in spite of the political origin of this movement, the deepest sources of power in the remarkable revolution lay in this appeal to nature, in this admonition to "consider the lilies of the field." Ikhnaton was a "God-intoxicated man," whose mind responded with marvelous sensitiveness and discernment to the visible evidences of God about him. He was fairly ecstatic in his sense of the beauty of the eternal and universal light. Its beams enfold him on every monument of his which has survived, and *only* him and his queen and the royal children, for he claims a unique relationship with his god. He prays, "May my eyes be satisfied daily with beholding him, when he dawns in this house of Aton and fills it with his own self by his beams, beauteous in love, and lays them upon me in satisfying life for ever and ever." In this light — which more than once, as here, he identifies with love, or again with beauty, as the visible evidence of the presence of God — he revels with an intoxication rarely to be found, and which may be properly compared to the ecstatic joy felt by such a soul as Ruskin in the contemplation of light. Ruskin, as he sees it playing over some lovely landscape, calls it "the breathing, animated, exulting light, which feels and receives and rejoices and acts — which chooses one thing and rejects another — which seeks and finds and loses again — leaping from rock to rock, from leaf to leaf, from wave to wave, glowing or flashing or scintillating according to what it strikes, or in its holier moods absorbing and enfolding all things in the deep fullness of its repose, and then again losing itself in bewilderment and doubt and dimness, or perishing and passing away, entangled in drifting mist, or melted into melancholy air, but still — kindling or declining, sparkling or still — it is the living light, which breathes in its deepest, most entranced rest, which sleeps but never dies." Here is modern ecstasy in the joyousness of light, a veritable gospel of the beauty of light, of which the earliest disciple was this lonely idealist of the fourteenth century before Christ. To Ikhnaton, too, the eternal light might sleep, when he that made the world has "gone to rest in his horizon," but to him also as with Ruskin it "sleeps but never dies." A badly broken passage in the great hymn has been successfully interpreted by Sethe as indicating that although the darkness had fallen and men slept, Ikhnaton could feel: "Yet art thou still in my heart."

In this aspect of Ikhnaton's movement, then, it is a gospel of the beauty and beneficence of the natural order, a recognition of the message of nature to the soul of man, which makes it the earliest of those revivals which we call in the case of such artists as Millet and the Barbizon school, or of Wordsworth and his successors, "a return to nature." The painters depict the wild life of the marshes with a new spirit different from the quiet pleasure of the mastaba painters of the Pyramid Age, whose serene pictures of the nobleman's excursions into the papyrus thickets adorn the walls of the tomb chapels in the Memphite cemetery at Sakkara. The frescoes which adorned the floor of Ikhnaton's colonnaded palace hall at Amarna are filled with a new joy of life, and we feel something of the passion which quickened the hand of the artist as in his mind's eye he saw the wild bull leaping in the papyrus thicket and tossing his head at the timorous birds twittering above the marsh reeds and scolding the ponderous intruder who is endangering their nests. Alas, that this noble painting, quivering with life and *movement* which long delighted the eyes of modern visitors at Amarna has now perished forever at the hands of modern native vandals from the neighbouring village!

This new spirit which drew its inspiration from the beauty and beneficence of *nature* was at the same time deeply sensitive to the life of *man* and to human relations as they actually were, undisturbed by convention or tradition. Ikhnaton's charmingly natural and unrestrained relations with his family were now depicted even on public monuments without reserve. A statuette found unfinished in a royal sculptor's studio at Amarna not only shows the king seated with his little daughter on his knee, as the royal father embraces the little princess, but depicts the Pharaoh in the very act of kissing the little girl as any normal father might do. It is not difficult to imagine the rage and horror which such a royal portrait excited in the feelings of the traditionalists of Ikhnaton's age, the conventional grandees of the court in whose eyes a Pharaoh should be depicted as he had been for two thousand years, an august presence seated in unbending majesty, a figure of divine immobility, unblemished by any evidence or suggestion of human feeling or human weakness. The lovely chair which came out of the palace at Amarna and has been preserved to us in the tomb of Tutenkhamon is adorned with a scene showing us the youthful king seated in a posture of negligent relaxation, with one arm thrown carelessly over the back of his chair, while the lovely young queen stands before him with a little jar of perfume in her hand, from which with exquisite grace she is touching her husband's costume with drops of fragrance. For the first time in the history of art, we have here a scene the subject of which is a *human relationship,* and interpretative art is here dealing with human life as its subject. These are but two among many examples which might be mentioned, which illustrate Ikhnaton's powerful individuality and his fearless readiness to throw off the shackles of tradition without hesitation in the endeavor to establish a world of things as they are, in wholesome naturalness.

It is important to notice, therefore, that Ikhnaton was a prophet both of nature and of human life. Like Jesus, who, on the one hand, drew his lessons from the lilies of the field, the fowls of the air, or the clouds of the sky, and, on the other, from the human society about him in stories like the Prodigal Son, the Good Samaritan, or the woman who had lost her piece of money, so this revolutionary Egyptian prophet drew his teachings from a contemplation both of nature and of human life. While the interpretative art of this revolutionary movement under Ikhnaton's guidance found *new* content in the life of man, there was much in Egyptian experience with human society which Ikhnaton could not ignore. He fully accepted the inherited Solar doctrine of a great moral order, and if in this brief history of Egyptian morals we have devoted some space to the revolutionary monotheism of Ikhnaton, it is for the reason that this whole monotheistic movement is the culmination of the ancient recognition of a moral order by the Egyptian thinkers of the Pyramid Age, and their creation of a realm of universal ethical values, represented by the inclusive term Maat, brought forth by the Sun-god at Heliopolis. This new monotheism grew up on a threefold basis. The *first,* as we have seen, was *political,* so that even the Sun-god's new name was enclosed in a Pharaonic double cartouche; the *second* was observation of the Sun-god's universal sway as a *physical force,* everywhere present in the sun's heat and light; and the *third* was the logical development of the ancient Heliopolitan doctrine of a *moral order,* a doctrine some two thousand years old in Ikhnaton's day.

We have still to consider the last of these fundamental bases of Ikhnaton's monotheism. It is at this point that we feel the insufficiency of our written sources, which are very meager. Even the scanty sources which have survived to us, however, disclose progress in the young king's thinking during the half generation of his rule. It is unthinkable that such a growing and progressing movement as that of Ikhnaton should not have produced treatises in which he set forth his doctrines. There is, moreover, good evidence of the existence of such writings. In the Amarna tombs where the nobles of Ikhnaton's court love to depict their relations with their sovereign, they constantly refer to the new faith. They have only one word for it, and that is the "teaching." It is attributed solely to the king, and we cannot doubt that this teaching is the general name for the formal statement of his doctrine in a treatise of some kind, written of course on papyrus. After his fall Ikhnaton's enemies left no stone unturned to obliterate every surviving evidence of his hated rule, and of course they destroyed these papyrus writings of the king. Our knowledge of the movement, as far as its tenets are concerned, is drawn exclusively from a few accidental scraps and fragments, especially the hymns with which the nobles embellished their tombs.

On first reading the great Aton hymn it seems remarkable that as an expression of religious aspiration such a hymn should contain so little reference to character and to human conduct, which as we know had held such a prominent place in the thinking of Solar religion at Heliopolis, and in which the entire Aton movement was deeply rooted. The source of this omission is to be found in the fact that the chief force which moved the soul of Ikhnaton was *emotion.* The Aton revolution was in spirit primarily and powerfully emotional. This fact is unmistakable in the hymns, and it is very prominent also in the art. When an Amarna artist sketches the worshipping figure of Ikhnaton or any of his subjects with arms "uplifted in adoration" to the Sun-god, the emotional quality of the lines with which he represents the uplifted arms is as powerfully appealing as the beseeching arms of Eleonora Duse outstretched to her beloved Armando. It is the beauty and beneficence of the Sun-god which Ikhnaton adores, and it is this emotion of which the Amarna hymns are the vehicle. They therefore contain no theology or social morality. Nevertheless it is quite clear that Ikhnaton fully accepted the highly developed ethics of Heliopolis, and indeed made the ethical system of the old Solar teaching more prominent than it had ever been before his reign.

The close connection of Ikhnaton's revolution with the Heliopolitan theology is evident throughout. The identification of the royal line with that of the Sun-god by the Heliopolitan priests in the Pyramid Age, making every Pharaoh a son of the Sun-god, had resulted, as we have seen, in transferring to Re the humane qualities of beneficent dominion with which the Pharaohs of the Feudal Age were imbued. At that time the Pharaoh had become the "good shepherd" or "good herdman," and this figure of the paternal and protecting sovereign had been transferred to Re. Re had thus gained wondrously in qualities of humane and paternal sympathy, as a result of this development in the conception of the kingship in the Feudal Age. The social forces which had contributed this high ideal of kingship were thus the ultimate influences, which, through the kingship, enriched and humanized the otherwise rather mechanical and perfunctory political conception of Re's dominion. The human appeal which he now made was thus akin to that of Osiris himself. The teaching of Ikhnaton was entirely in sympathy with this tendency of the Solar faith. Under his father we have found a sun-hymn calling the Sun-god "the valiant herdman driving his herds," a hint clearly connecting the Aton faith with the social and moral movement of the Feudal Age.

Recalling now the Heliopolitan origin of Maat, "justice," "truth," "righteousness," personified as a goddess, the daughter of the Sun-god, it is important to notice that in the Book of the Dead (Chapter cxxv) we find a group of the gods who sit in the "Hall of Maat, in whose bodies are neither sin nor falsehood, who live in truth (Maat)." To these gods the deceased asserts, "I live on truth, I feed on the truth (or "righteousness") of my heart." Now this Solar doctrine maintained by the gods at Heliopolis was so fully accepted by Ikhnaton that he regularly appended to the official form of his royal name in all his great state monuments, the words "Living on Truth" (Maat). This significant epithet attached to Ikhnaton's name proclaimed him the official representative and supporter of the great moral and national order conceived by the Solar priests at Heliopolis as far back as the Pyramid Age and given ever deeper ethical significance by the social thinkers and prophets of the Feudal Age. When we recall Ikhnaton's unqualified claim to universal dominion, it is evident that by appending these words to his royal name he intended to extend the old *national* moral order to exercise sway over the greater *international* world of which he was lord. The Sun-god's ancient realm of ethical values, expanded to its logical universal limits and the monotheism long ago implicit in the teaching of the priests of Heliopolis, was thus given unequivocal expression by Ikhnaton.

In harmony with this fact Ikhnaton called his new capital at Amarna the "seat of truth" (Maat) in the short hymn. His partisans were fully aware of the king's convictions regarding Maat, and we frequently find the men of his court glorifying "truth." One of his leading supporters, Eye, who later displaced Tutenkhamon as king, says: "He [the king] put truth in my body and my abomination is lying. I know that Wanre [Ikhnaton] rejoices in it [truth]." The same man affirms that the Sun-god is one "[whose] heart is satisfied with truth, whose abomination is falsehood." Another official states in his Amarna tomb: "I will speak to his majesty, [for] I know that he lives therein. . . . I do not that which his majesty hates, [for] my abomination is lying in my body. . . . I have reported truth to his majesty, [for] I know that he lives therein. Thou art Re, begetter of truth . . . I took not the reward of lying, nor expelled the truth for the violent." As important evidence of Ikhnaton's devotion to truth it should be recalled here that he did not confine truth to conduct only, but introduced it also into the realm of *art* with epoch-making results.

In Ikhnaton's revolution, therefore, Re was still the author and sustainer of truth or righteousness (Maat), the moral and administrative order, as he had been for over two thousand years before, and if we hear of no judgment hereafter in the Amarna tombs, it was clearly only the rejection of the cloud of gods and demi-gods, with Osiris at their head, who had been involved in the judgment as we find it in the Book of the Dead. These were now banished, and the dramatic scene of the judgment seems to have disappeared with them, although it is clear that the ethical requirements of the Solar faith, the faith in which they emerged and developed, were not relaxed in Ikhnaton's teaching. The sacerdotal invasion of the moral realm with mechanical magical agencies for insuring justification was also evidently repelled by Ikhnaton. The familiar heart scarab now no longer bears a charm to still the accusing voice of conscience, but a simple prayer, in the name of Aton, for long life, favor and food. The same was true of the Ushebti figures, the little images which performed labor in the deceased's stead in the hereafter.

On a moment's reflection, such fundamental changes as these suggest what an overwhelming tide of inherited thought, custom, and tradition had been diverted from its channel by the young king who was guiding this revolution. It is only as this aspect of his movement is clearly discerned that we begin to appreciate the power of his remarkable personality. Before his time religious documents were commonly attributed to ancient kings and wise men, and the power of a belief lay chiefly in its claim to remote antiquity and the sanctity of immemorial custom. Until Ikhnaton the history of the world had largely been merely the irresistible drift of tradition. The outstanding exception was the great physician-architect, Imhotep, who introduced stone architecture and built the first stone masonry pyramidal tomb of the thirtieth century B.C. Otherwise men had been but drops of water in the great current. With the possible exception of Imhotep, Ikhnaton was the first individual in history. Consciously and deliberately, by intellectual process, he gained his position and then placed himself squarely in the face of tradition and swept it aside. He appeals to no myths, to no ancient and widely accepted versions of the dominion of the gods, to no customs sanctified by centuries — he appeals only to the present and visible evidences of his god's dominion, evidences open to all, and as for tradition wherever it had left material manifestations of other gods in records which could be reached, he endeavored to annihilate it. A policy so destructive was doomed to encounter fatal opposition.

Was Akhnaton a Monotheist?

JOHN A. WILSON

John A. Wilson was born in Pawling, New York in 1899; he was educated at the Universities of Chicago, Berlin, and Munich. In 1926 he became Professor of Egyptology at Chicago University's Oriental Institute.

THE MOST IMPORTANT observation about Amarna religion is that there were two gods central to the faith, and not one. Akh-en-Aton and his family worshipped the Aton, and everybody else worshipped Akh-en-Aton *as a god*. In addition to his formal names and titles, the pharaoh was referred to as "the good god," and he asserted that he was the physical son of the Aton. The abundant scenes in the Amarna tombs show him serving the living sun-disk, while all of his courtiers bow in adoration to him. Their prayers were not addressed to the Aton, but directly to Akh-en-Aton. The courtier Eye, who was later to become pharaoh, asked Akh-en-Aton for mortuary benefits: "Mayest thou grant to me a good old age as thy favorite; mayest thou grant to me a goodly burial by the command of thy *ka* in my house. . . . May (I) hear thy sweet voice in the sanctuary when thou performest that which pleases thy father, the living Aton." Another noble did pray to the Aton, but prayed only on behalf of Akh-en-Aton, with his petition for himself addressed to the pharaoh: "Mayest thou make thy beloved son Akh-en-Aton to live with thee forever, [to do] what thy heart [wishes], and to behold what thou dost every day, for he rejoices in the sight of thy beauty. . . . Let him (remain) here, until the swan turns black, until the raven turns white, until the mountains stand up to walk, and until the sea runs up the river. And may I continue in service of the good god (Akh-en-Aton), until he assigns (to me) the burial that he gives." This is a stated acknowledgement of the centrality of the pharaoh in the worship of the Aton and of the dependence of the noble upon his god-king.

Akh-en-Aton himself in his famous hymn to the Aton asserted that this was his personal god. The hymn is entitled "the worship of the Aton . . . by the King Akh-en-Aton and the Queen Nefert-iti," and pharaoh says explicitly: "Thou art in my heart, and there is no other that knows thee except thy son (Akh-en-Aton), whom thou hast initiated into thy plans and into thy power." It must be emphasized that the Aton faith had no penetration below the level of the royal family as an effective religious expression; it was stated to be the exclusive faith of the god-king and his divine family, and the god-king welcomed and encouraged his subjects' worship of his divine being as the source of all the benefits which they might desire.

The self-centered nature of Akh-en-Aton's faith, the fact that only the royal family had a trained and reasoned loyalty to the Aton, and the fact that all of pharaoh's adherents were forced to give their entire devotion to him as a god-king explain why the new religion collapsed after Akh-en-Aton's death. Political and economic factors were also important, but the observation that the Amarna courtiers had contact with the Aton only through their worship of Akh-en-Aton shows the fleeting and superficial nature of the religion. We cannot believe that they cherished within their bosoms the teaching about a benevolent and sustaining sole god, the Aton, when all of their religious exercise was exhausted in worship of Akh-en-Aton. When that pharaoh died and the movement collapsed, they must have scrambled penitently back into the traditional faith, which they could understand and in which they were allowed wider devotion.

Two important questions face us. Was this monotheism? If so, was it the world's first ancestral monotheism, and did it come down to us through the Hebrews? Our own answer to each question is in the negative, even though such an answer may rest upon definitions of the terms, and such definitions must necessarily be those of modern distinctions.

Our modern Jewish, Christian, and Moslem faiths express the doctrine that there is one — and only one — God and that all ethical and religious values derive from that God. In the application of this definition to the Amarna religion, we see that there were at least two gods, that the Aton was concerned strictly with creating and maintaining life, and that ethics and religion derived from the pharaoh Akh-en-Aton.

It is true that the Amarna texts call the Aton the "sole god, like whom there is no other." This, however, was nothing new in Egyptian religious address. The form of expression was a fervid exaggeration or concentration, which went back to the earliest religious literature, more than a thousand years before Akh-en-Aton's time. In the period before the Amarna revolution, Amon, Re, Atum, Har-akhti, and Min were severally called "the sole god." Sometimes this term recalled the creation, when the one existent god was going to bring other gods into being. Sometimes it was a flattering exaggeration meaning the only important god, *like whom* there was no other. Often it was a focusing of the worshipper's attention upon one god, to the exclusion of others — what is called henotheism or mo-

nolatry. In no sense does it imply the absolute unity carried by the Moslem: "There is no god but God."

In ancient times a man's name was a vital part of his being: the effacing of his name from his tomb destroyed his continued existence in the next world; the expunging of an official's name from the records ended that earthly success which was so important to his survival. The same psychology applies to Akh-en-Aton's attack upon Amon and topically upon other gods. If the philosophy of the new religion was that only the Aton was a god and that, therefore, Amon did not and could not exist, why was there so virulent an attack upon Amon, and why was his name systematically hacked out of the records? In those ancient terms he had still some kind of existence as long as his name was effectively a part of a single record.

We are conscious that we are arguing in modern terms and that Atonism was at one and the same time native to Egyptian religion and unique within that religion. It was native because the Egyptian state was built upon the dogma that pharaoh was a god and stood between the people and the other gods; thus the double relationship at Amarna retained the past essentials. It was unique because the gods other than pharaoh were made one god, by a process of exclusion rather than syncretism, if we ignore that limited syncretism present in the official names of the Aton. It is immaterial to that argument that there was still personification in the texts, by which the Aton was described as "satisfied with the goddess Ma'at" and Akh-en-Aton was praised as being "the god Fate," because personification was also native to Egyptian thought. Much more important was the elimination of Osiris from the mortuary faith, with the ascription of all mortuary benefits to the pharaoh. One could say that it was the closest approach to monotheism possible within the thought of the day. That would still fall short of making it a belief in and worship of only one god.

The question as to whether Atonism was

ancestral to Hebrew monotheism and thus to modern expressions of religion is also difficult. However, it may be stated flatly that the mechanism of transmission from the faith of Akh-en-Aton to the monotheism of Moses is not apparent. This was the personal religion of a pharaoh who later became a heretic within one generation. It was not accessible to Egyptians at large. Their subsequent reaction in a fervent return to the older forms, particularly the Osirian faith and the cherishing care of little personal gods, shows how little penetration Atonism had below the royal family. Even assuming that there were Israelite slave troops in Egypt in Amarna times, there was no way by which they could learn the teaching of Atonism, that there was a single, universal god, who made and continued life, toward whom the worshipper felt a warm sense of gratitude. Atonism taught that the pharaoh of Egypt was essential as the only intermediary between god and people.

There is another discontinuity between Atonism and Hebrew monotheism as the latter developed, and that is the marked lack of ethical content in the hymns directed to the Aton. Akh-en-Aton's faith was intellectual rather than ethical; its strong emotional content derived from the fervor of the discoverer and convert, who rejected past forms and preached new forms. The conviction of right and wrong was not ethical, but was a passionate reiteration that the new was right and the old was wrong. Aton's blessings were primarily physical; he made and sustained life. The worshipper was called upon to render gratitude for that life, but was in no text called upon to render to the god an upright and ethically correct life in his social relations or in his innermost heart. The universalism of the Aton could have carried the implication that all men are equal under the god and should be so treated, but such a logical conclusion is strikingly absent from the texts.

The one point of question against this description of Atonism as nature worship lies in the understanding of *ma'at* empha-

sized by this faith. Akh-en-Aton lived on *ma'at* as his food, and the Aton was satisfied with *ma'at* as his offering. If this meant "righteousness" or "justice," it would carry an ethical weight. When, however, we see in scenes and texts the emphasis on candid relations, on the open air, and on adoration of the sun-disk, we can only translate it as "truth" and understand it as the worship of the forces of nature, in contradistinction to the remote and artificial activity of the older gods. Nowhere do we find that rigorous insistence upon law which was central in Hebrew monotheism.

There is a more important consideration about the transmission of monotheism from one culture to another, and that is whether any great intellectual, spiritual, or ethical concept can be passed from one culture to quite a different culture. We have argued that the Egyptians were "civilized" in a sense of the word which has both strength and weakness. Much of the importance of the Hebrews to world history lies in the fact that they avoided some of the weakening and distracting phases of civilization. A concept which was imperfectly articulated and understood at pharaoh's court at Amarna would have been quite foreign to Asiatic tribes wandering in the desert. When the Children of Israel penetrated Canaan and settled down to work out a new way of life, their progressive religious steps were achieved through their own national religious experience as their own God-given discoveries, without derivation from any foreign source. Such precious and inner expressions of religion can never be borrowed, but must be experienced. When they have been experienced, the *forms* in which they are uttered may be borrowed from others, but never the innermost spirit.

This brings us to a main argument for the contact between Atonism and Hebrew religion: the extraordinary parallelism in thought and structure between Akh-en-Aton's hymn to the Aton and the 104th Psalm. Three selected passages will illustrate the striking similarity.

THE ATON HYMN	PSALM 104
When thou settest in the western horizon, The land is in darkness like death. . . . Every lion comes forth from his den;	Thou makest darkness and it is night,
All creeping things, they sting.	Wherein all the beasts of the forest creep forth. The young lions roar after their prey.
At daybreak, when thou arisest in the horizon . . . Thou drivest away the darkness . . . Men awake and stand upon their feet . . . All the world, they do their labor.	The sun ariseth, they get them away . . .
	Man goeth forth unto his work, And to his labor until the evening.
How manifold are thy works! They are hidden from man's sight. O sole god, like whom there is no other, Thou hast made the earth according to thy desire.	O Jahweh, how manifold are thy works!
	In wisdom hast thou made them all;
	The earth is full of thy riches.

It has been claimed that such correspondences must show derivative connection and that the Hebrew psalmists must have known the Egyptian sun-hymn. Since the obliteration of Atonism was complete some six or seven centuries before the psalm was written, it is argued that the Aton hymn must have passed into Asia when Akh-en-Aton was still in power and escaped destruction by translation into some Semitic dialect.

So ingenious a mechanism of transmission is not necessary. We have already seen that the several ideas and modes of expression visible in Atonism were present in Egypt before Atonism and independent of Atonism. Since these were current forms in Egypt, not invented by the Amarna priests or scribes, it is not surprising to find them still in use after the fall of Atonism and without relation to the fact that the specific cult had been proclaimed a heresy.

A papyrus in Leyden dates from the Nineteenth Dynasty and has passages which have been called monotheistic, but which we, with a narrower definition, prefer to call syncretistic. These hymns treat the god Amon as the summation of all other important gods, without rejecting the separate existence of those other gods.

Mysterious of form, glistening of appearance, the marvelous god of many forms. All

gods boast of him, to magnify themselves through his beauty, according as he is divine. Re himself is united with his body, and he is the great one who is in Heliopolis. He is called Ta-tenen (of Memphis) and Amon who came forth from Nun. . . . Another of his forms is the Eight (primeval gods of Hermopolis). . . . His soul, they say, is that which is in heaven, but it is he who is in the underworld and presides over the east. His soul is in heaven, his body is in the west, and his statue is in Hermonthis, heralding his appearances (to mankind). . . . One is Amon, hiding himself from them, concealing himself from (other) gods, so that his (very) color is unknown. He is far from heaven, he is absent from (?) the underworld, and no (other) god knows his true form. . . . All gods are three: Amon, Re, and Ptah, and there is no second to them. "Hidden" is his name as Amon, he is Re in face, and his body is Ptah. . . . Only he is: Amon, with Re, [and with Ptah] — together three.

Another set of hymns dating from the late Nineteenth or the Twentieth Dynasty treats Amon as a universal god, who again achieves unity by borrowing the forms of other gods. As the creator-god, he is Amon-Re-Atum-Har-akhti, four in one, or is Ptah, the fashioner of men. He delights in assuming functional roles. "His love is (to play the role of) the moon, as a child to whom everybody dances. . . . His love is (to play the role of) Har-akhti shining in the horizon of heaven." He is both the son and father of *ma'at*, the "truth" which destroys deceit: "Thy mother is Ma'at, O Amon! She belongs uniquely to thee, and she came forth from thee (already) inclined to rage and burn up them that attack thee. Ma'at is more unique, O Amon, than anyone that exists." He is the universal creator, "who spoke with his mouth and there came into existence all men, gods, large and small cattle in their entirety, and all that which flies and lights." He is the warmer and sustainer of all nature: "Green plants turn about in his direction, that they may be beautiful, and lotuses are gay because of him." He is the good shepherd: "Thou are valiant as a herdsman tending them forever and ever. . . . Their hearts turn about to thee, good at all times. Everybody lives through the sight of thee."

We shall see that artistic forms and themes survived the condemnation of the Amarna movement, and it is equally true that religious concepts and forms of expression continued after Atonism had been made a heresy. This is an adequate explanation of the similarity between the Aton hymn and the 104th Psalm. Hymns of this kind were current long after the fall of Akhen-Aton, so that when Hebrew religion had reached a point where it needed a certain mode of expression it could find in another literature phrases and thoughts which would meet the need.

The negative statement which we have made about the Aton religion has been argumentative and fails to do justice to the elements of supreme importance in that faith. To be sure, it was intellectual and lacking in full ethical value. At the same time, it expressed beautifully the concept of a god who was creative, nurturing, and kindly and who gave his gifts to all mankind and to all living things everywhere and not to the Egyptians alone. For such bounty the worshipper returned gratitude and devotion to the god. Atonism further brought religion out into the open and tried to end the remoteness and secrecy of the old cults of the powerful and wealthy gods. It was a major tragedy that a religion of such broad intellectual scope lacked the inner moral warmth to give it permanency. The fuller realization of the meaning of God's cherishing care was to be made by other and later peoples.

IV. THE FREUDIAN HYPOTHESIS

A Review of Freud

SALO W. BARON

Born in 1895 in Tarnow, Austria, Salo W. Baron has been Professor of Jewish History at Columbia University since 1930. He is also Director of Columbia's Center of Israeli Studies and the author of a multi-volume *Social and Religious History of the Jews.*

IF A THINKER of Sigmund Freud's stature takes a stand on a problem of vital interest to him, the world is bound to listen. If the work so produced is also a remarkable human and historical document, if unwittingly it is a reflection of the profound changes in the entire mental atmosphere of Central Europe during the last decade, the reader's intellectual curiosity will receive stimuli in fields transcending the vast and ramified subject treated therein. Its first two — smaller — sections, which merely adumbrated the major theme, were published in 1937 in the German journal *Imago.* But the main Part III, which in the author's words "reduces religion to the status of a neurosis of mankind and explains its grandiose powers in the same way as we should a neurotic obsession in our individual patients," appeared too full of dynamite for an author living under the Catholic regime of Dollfuss and Schuschnigg. Its final composition had to await the conquest of Austria by Hitler, the subsequent persecution of Freud on ideological as well as racial grounds, and his escape to England, which, although far more Christian than either Austria or Germany, bears with much greater composure a psychoanalytical critique of the Christian dogma. To be sure, this unusual genesis of the work has resulted in considerable technical shortcomings and endless repetitions. Freud himself, hitherto a master of literary presentation which but a few years ago had rightly earned for him the major Goethe prize in contemporary German literature, deeply deplores these shortcomings, which make his discussion "as ineffectual as it is inartistic." Inartistic, yes — but far from ineffectual. If anything, the constant hammering of a few *leitmotifs* helps to impress upon the reader's mind those views of the author which at first appear to him farfetched or even repugnant, and to evoke the impression of certainty and logical cogency where, by the very nature of the subject, everything is so profoundly uncertain and hypothetical.

The subject of Moses and the origins of monotheism lends itself, like few others in the history of religion, to extensive, analytical treatment. The availability of a fairly large body of biographic and ethnological material, principally in the Bible, is enhanced by the great chronological gap between the events narrated therein and their record in its present form which makes it open to an endless variety of interpretation.

Reprinted from *"Moses and Monotheism* by Sigmund Freud — a Book Review," by Salo W. Baron, *The American Journal of Sociology,* XLV, no. 3 (November, 1939), 471–477, by permission of The University of Chicago Press.

A great deal of further folkloristic material, some of it doubtless also containing a kernel of historical truth, has been preserved in the more articulate, but still younger rabbinic and patristic, literatures, of which Freud — perhaps to his credit — has made but little use. The well-known lack of agreement among modern biblical scholars and anthropologists on some of the most fundamental issues likewise equips the analytical investigator with a mass of alternative suggestions from which he may choose those which best fit into the pattern of his theory. "The more shadowy tradition has become," says Freud, "the more meet is it for the poet's use." Nevertheless, perhaps as a result of being too much earth-bound and source-bound, the present reviewer feels that he cannot quite follow the author into this rarefied atmosphere of pure speculation.

In this new work Freud elaborates and illustrates, by the specific example of Moses, his main thesis on the development of religion which he had first advanced in 1912 in his striking volume on *Totem and Taboo*. In its bare essentials the theory assumes a parallelism between the evolution of mankind from its prehistoric stages to contemporary civilization and the individual growth of man from childhood to adult life. Just as in individual life the first five years after birth leave permanent impressions which, carried through a period of sexual latency to the age of pubescence, definitely condition adult psychic life and lay the ground for all human neuroses, so is mankind at large carrying in its subconscious mind the heritage of its all-important formative stage. Although forgotten during the long subsequent period of latency, the impressions of this prehistoric stage time and again come to the fore in the consciousness of civilized man. Following suggestions made by Darwin and Atkinson, Freud has long advocated the hypothesis that mankind had begun its career as a father horde, in which one strong male was the master and father of the whole horde. Unlimited in his power, he appropriated all females

and banished all males outside the horde. At last a group of such exiled brothers "clubbed together, overcame the father, and — according to the custom of those times — all partook of his body." Of course, each of these brothers deeply desired to inherit the mantle which had thus fallen from the revered father's shoulders, but unable to overcome the resistance of the others and realizing that internecine fights were as dangerous as they were futile, compromised upon a new form of a social organization based upon the recognition of mutual obligations. These were the beginnings of morality and law. Instead of each appropriating the women of the horde to himself, the brothers renounced them altogether and established exogamy as their guiding principle. They also found a substitute for the father in a totem, usually an animal, revered as the father of the tribe which, in memory of what had happened to the primeval father, no one was allowed to kill, but which on a stated occasion was consumed in a sacrificial repast. The new leaders of the brother-horde thus

undid their deed by declaring that the killing of the father substitute, the totem, was not allowed, and renounced the fruit of their deed by denying themselves the liberated women. Thus they created two fundamental taboos of totemism out of the *sense of guilt of the son*, and for this very reason these had to correspond with the two repressed wishes of the Oedipus complex. Whoever disobeyed became guilty of the two only crimes which troubled primitive society.

Animal worship was subsequently replaced by human deities, just as socially the matriarchate gave way to a re-established patriarchal organization. But the dim memories of that early eventful revolution, after a period of latency, came back to haunt man, who by that time had attained a high degree of material and intellectual civilization.

For reasons which cannot fully be explained, in the fourteenth century B.C., under the reign of the Egyptian king, Ikhnaton, these memories blossomed out into the first, and perhaps purest, form of a monotheistic creed. The details of Ikhnaton's memorable reform, its antecedents in the doctrines of the priests of the Sun Temple at On, the influences emanating from Syria, perhaps through the king's Syrian wives, and the impact of Egyptian imperialism can no longer be ascertained, because the successful opposition after 1350 B.C. destroyed nearly all pertinent records. In any case, however, it apparently would have remained but an interesting historical episode were it not for the work of one of Ikhnaton's Egyptian disciples, named Moses. Freud, after repeating many older arguments in favor of Moses' Egyptian origin, adds an interesting psychoanalytic explanation of the Moses legend. As Otto Rank had shown some thirty years ago, this legend closely corresponds to a very widespread type of hero myth, except in one essential point, viz., that here the hero actually came from the noble rather than from the humble family in the story. Some time after 1350 B.C. this Egyptian prince, perhaps also governor of the province of Goshen, where a large number of Israelites had been living under Egyptian domination, tried to salvage the suppressed teachings of Ikhnaton by creating a new following among these Semitic settlers, taking them out of Egypt and leading them to Palestine. In southern Palestine the new arrivals, as yet unprepared for the high spirituality of the new religion, murdered their leader — Freud takes here a clue from a fantastic "discovery" of Ernst Sellin — and joined a number of closely related tribes which had settled there before. Together the two groups soon came under the sway of another leader whom we may conveniently designate as the Midianite Moses. This dualism of two religions and two founders, like the other dualities of Jewish history — two peoples forming one nation, its breaking up into two kingdoms, and the two names of the Deity — is the necessary consequence of the fact that "one section of the people passed through what may properly be termed a traumatic experience

which the other was spared." After the Egyptian Moses' death this, so to say, childhood experience of the Jewish people entered once more a period of relative latency, during which only a small minority of Levites, descendants of the original small circle of native Egyptians around Moses, carried on the tradition of the lawgiver. Several centuries later, under the stimulus of the Israelitic prophets, the original Mosaic religion was reestablished as the national religion of Israel. This monotheistic creed thus became the revived memory of the primeval father. "The great deed or misdeed of primeval times, the murder of the father, was brought home to the Jews, for fate decreed that they should repeat it on the person of Moses, an eminent father substitute." With their new belief in God, the Father, went the expectation of the return of the lawgiver, as the Messiah — Freud could have used here another hypothesis of Sellin, since abandoned, that the expected Messiah of early Israelitic prophecy was Moses redivivus, a belief held long after by Samaritan schismatics — the conviction of Israel's chosenness, and most of the teachings of ancient Judaism, including imageless worship, ritualism, growth of spirituality, and circumcision. The latter custom, clearly of Egyptian origin, was unwittingly taken over by Moses because of its inherent connection with the castration complex originating from the relations between the primeval father and his sons. This Mosaic restoration of the primeval father still left some parts of the prehistoric tragedy unrecognized, however. Operating underground for several more centuries, they gradually generated that widespread feeling of guilt which characterized both the Jewish people and the entire Mediterranean world at the beginning of the Christian era. This sense of guilt once more resulted in the murder of a leader, but this time it was the Son who died in expiation for the primeval murder of the Father. This is, according to Freud, the underlying motif for Paul's doctrine of the original sin, just as the Christian communion is but a resurgence of the bodily partaking of the primeval father and its derivative, the sacrificial repast of the totem cults. Through the Crucifixion, on the other hand, the Christian religion truly became but a Son religion, and hence its triumph "was a renewed victory of the Ammon priests over the God of Ikhnaton." The Jewish people who, "with its usual stiff-necked obduracy," continued to deny the murder of their "father," consequently suffered severe persecution. The accusation of Christ-killing really means "You won't admit that you murdered God" (the primeval father and his reincarnations), whereas "we did the same thing, but we admitted it, and since then we have been purified."

This bold and ingenious reconstruction of the history of religion, of which a bare, and in many respects incomplete, outline has been presented here, is supported by a great many detailed, no less bold and ingenious, observations which make the book worthwhile reading even for one who will ultimately disagree with its main thesis. Methodically, however, the work is open to most crucial objections. The extreme liberties admittedly taken by Freud with available biblical material are illustrative also of his utilization of the findings of modern anthropological and historical research.

When I use Biblical tradition here in such an autocratic and arbitrary way, draw on it for confirmation whenever it is convenient, and dismiss its evidence without scruple when it contradicts my conclusions, I know full well that I am exposing myself to severe criticism concerning my method and that I weaken the force of my proofs. But this is the only way in which to treat material whose trustworthiness — as we know for certain — was seriously damaged by the influence of distorting tendencies.

Many of us, unfortunately, will have to disagree. No, this is not the only way; it is not even the way of authors such as A. Allwohn who, with the help of psychoanalysis, has tried to reconstruct the subconscious erotic motivations of the prophetic career of Hosea, a subject, it may readily be granted, much more promising than that of the austere figure of Moses in the biblical tradition. This limitless arbitrariness in the selection and use of the little existing evidence renders the entire factual basis of Freud's reconstruction more than questionable. The primeval-father horde and the murder of the primeval father are considered by almost all contemporary anthropologists as a figment of imagination. The explanation of the subsequent rise of totemism, based upon a suggestion once made by W. Robertson Smith, is here upheld by Freud even though he knows that "more recent ethnologists have without exception discarded" Smith's theories. For the career of the historical Moses, he quotes outstanding modern scholars — Meyer, Gressman, Sellin, Breasted — of whom he speaks with greater awe than of the original biblical sources and ancient monuments. But he selects from these writers some of their most fantastic views, often timidly advanced and sometimes later revoked by the authors themselves, drags them out of their context, and combines them into a new artificial entity. The factual evidence for the Egyptian origin of Moses largely reduces itself to the etymology of the name, but this proof appears no more conclusive than would be a parallel attempt to deduce from the name Zerubbabel, the leader of another exodus of Jewish exiles, that he was a native Babylonian. The Jews have probably then, as ever after, adopted the names prevalent among the national majorities in the midst of whom they chanced to live. Wholly untenable is Freud's attempt at identification of the divine name, *Adonai*, in Israel's credo with the Egyptian Aton. The Deuteronomic source has, of course, *Yahwe*. The substitute, *Adonai*, and its Greek equivalent, *kyrios*, are first clearly indicated in the Hellenistic period, a millennium after Moses. Neither is the violent death of Moses more than a farfetched hypothesis, largely given up by its author and shared by no other biblical scholar. Similar objections could easily be raised also against many other essential links in the Freudian reconstruction. Even if the entire factual background were proved beyond peradventure, however, as it is not, the old question would still remain as to whether the Freudian parallelism between individual and mass psychology (assuming the correct interpretation of the former) can be scientifically upheld. The period of latency, particularly, which in the case of the lapse of time between the alleged murder of the primeval father and the appearance of Ikhnaton would extend over countless generations, presupposes an extent of transmission of memories through some sort of heredity which, Freud himself admits, is unequivocally rejected "by the present attitude of biological science." In short, the cause of psychoanalytical interpretation of the history of religion, brilliantly initiated by Freud and his disciples several decades ago, seems to the present reviewer to have

received a setback rather than to have made further progress through its present application to the historical career of Moses.

These considerations will probably carry little weight with "that minority of readers familiar with analytical reasoning and able to appreciate its conclusions," to which the author, notwithstanding his sincere efforts at popularization, primarily addresses himself. To many of these initiates, the present work, despite its scientific argumentation, will appeal as the pronunciamento of a revered prophet and sectarian leader, entirely immune from the so-called rational, but essentially psychically conditioned and hence prejudiced, attacks by outsiders. To the outsiders (and the present reviewer professes to be one of them), however, much as they may admire the author's erudition and dialectical prowess, this ingenious structure will appear as but a magnificent castle in the air.

A Question of Method

H. L. PHILP

The Reverend Canon Philp, born in 1902, has long been a lecturer in social psychology at Exeter University College in his native England. The author of *Jung and the Problem of Evil*, he has written frequently on the relationship between psychology and religion.

"But we venture to be independent of the historians in other respects and to blaze our own trail."

SIGMUND FREUD,
Moses and Monotheism (p. 60)

FREUD'S LAST BOOK was concerned with the subject in which, during the latter part of his life, he had shown so great an interest — religion. For many years he had

planned a vast work which would apply psychoanalytical theories to the whole of the Bible. *Moses and Monotheism* was the only part of it which he was able to complete. He had always been particularly interested in Moses, and when he visited Rome he was fascinated by Michelangelo's famous statue and wrote a paper on this subject in 1914 which, curiously enough, he published anonymously.

From H. L. Philp, *Freud and Religious Belief* (London: Barrie and Rockliff Publishing Corporation, 1956), pp. 92–95, 106–123. Reprinted by permission of the publishers.

The theme of *Moses and Monotheism* is an astonishing one, even for a Jew who did not accept the faith of his fathers. Briefly it is as follows: Moses was not a Jew but an Egyptian, and Jewish monotheism was derived from Egypt, in particular from a period of pure monotheism established during the reign of Ikhnaton. Freud believed that Moses was the son, presumably illegitimate, of one of the daughters of a Pharaoh, and that he lived in Egypt during the period immediately following Ikhnaton. Because of his birth he was a person of great importance; possibly he had been governor of a province and as such had come into touch with the Israelites. In his zeal as a reformer Ikhnaton had attempted to stamp out the popular religion, and after his death there was a tremendous revolt against all that he had stood for. Moses was an adherent of Ikhnaton, but because of the revolution he was not able to practise, at least openly, the form of religion in which he believed. He therefore decided to free the Israelites from Egypt and to train them in the monotheistic religion of Ikhnaton. This he did, but after a period (it is not known how long) the Israelites revolted and killed him. After at least two generations, and probably somewhat longer, the Israelites had another leader to whom also they gave the name of Moses and it was he, the second Moses, who gave them their Yahweh religion. But the teaching of the first Moses, the Egyptian, remained a latent force in the racial unconscious of the Israelites and was responsible for the monotheism of the prophets and people hundreds of years later. In fact it was only then that the teaching of the first Moses emerged in all its purity.

In the killing of the first Moses we have another example of the slaying of the primal father, and a sense of guilt about it remained in the racial unconscious. The significance of the death of Jesus was that it was an atonement by one of the brothers for the slaying of the father. Salvation was obtained through the sacrifice of Jesus, and Christianity became a religion based on the

son rather than on the stern father. The Holy Communion has the importance of the primitive totem feast and is in a direct line of descent from it.

Biblical and other scholars who have studied this period are well aware of the problems connected with Moses, the Exodus and its date, the different views about the period of Ikhnaton's reign and the development of Hebrew monotheism. These are realms in which there is ample room for speculation and Freud speculated to the full. Indeed he himself wrote, in discussing the supposed murder of the first Moses and the date of a second Moses, "as we know that in our hypothesis one assumption only rests on another we have to admit that this discussion shows a weak spot in the construction." Anyone who has studied the processes of perception knows that where the field of perception is ambiguous there is the greatest variation in what is seen. The deciding factor is usually what is expected or desired, a fact recognized and taken advantage of by every conjuror. By the unconscious selection of the most unlikely hypotheses, and the ignoring of all material which was contrary to his main contentions, Freud produced a thesis which appeared to him to be convincing as an exposition of the theories of psychoanalysis applied to this particular realm.

The general consensus of opinion among scholars in this field is well expressed by one of the most eminent of them, W. F. Albright, in his *From the Stone Age to Christianity* ("Monotheism and the Historical Process"):

As a counterpoise to these serious, though exaggerated, theories we may be pardoned for saying a word about a futile but widely read example of psychological determinism — Freud's *Moses and Monotheism* (1939). This book is simply the latest of a long train of books and papers on history and religion which have been issued by Freud himself and other members of the psychoanalytical school during the past generation. Like them his new book is totally devoid of serious historical method and deals with historical data even more cavalierly than with the data of introspective and experimental psychology.

Allowance must be made, of course, for the conditions under which this book was written. Parts I and II were published in German in 1937 when Freud was over eighty, and nearly the whole of Part III was rewritten in London from June, 1938, and although this was more than half the whole book it was completed within about six weeks after his arrival — according to a report published by H. W. Puner. During the planning of the book in Vienna he was surrounded by bitter anti-Semitism. His books were burnt and his publishing house destroyed; his whole future and that of his children were in danger. There was every kind of disturbance and a real fear of persecution, and in the middle of the writing of this book came the move to England. As if this were not enough there was the long-standing and painful cancer of the mouth and, of course, there was old age. All these things must have had their effect and are at least partly responsible for the fact that this is the most ill-arranged, discursive, repetitive and unconvincing of all his works.

* * *

It would seem that Freud not only exaggerated the place of Ikhnaton as a religious reformer, but that he probably simplified the Egyptian religion of the period, especially when he called it "pure monotheism."

The sun always had a dominating place in Egyptian thought and life because of its practical, powerful, day-to-day influence. It might be thought that with so much sun the darkness would be welcomed as giving protection. In fact the Egyptians hated darkness and they found their happiness in greeting the rising of the sun which was viewed as a source of light and life, and gradually the personification of the sun's power led to the belief in the sun-god who became the supreme creator god. There were other gods, but the sun, as the supreme god, lent himself to other gods to give "them a primacy within geographical or functional limits."

Wilson believes that "the fluidity of Egyptian concepts and the tendency to synthesize divergent elements" has been responsible for the contention that the Egyptians were monotheistic, that all the gods were subsumed into a single god. But he believes too that such views are wrong in that they simplify the actual position far too much, for "it is not a matter of single god but of single nature of observed phenomena in the universe, with the clear possibility of exchange and substitution. With relation to gods and men the Egyptians were monophysites: many men and many gods, but all ultimately of one nature."

Although the Egyptians recognized different beings they felt that they were of a single essential substance, "a rainbow, in which certain colours were dominant under certain conditions and others dominant when the conditions altered. A complete personality includes many different aspects of personality."

Meek in *Hebrew Origins* gives his verdict both about Ikhnaton and his possible influence on monotheism:

Instead of helping the cause of monotheism Akhenaten killed it by bringing the Egyptian movement toward monotheism to a head too soon, by making too great a break with the old religion, by resorting to force to establish his religion, and by dying too soon, leaving no efficient successor to carry on his work. If Akhenaten was not able to convert his own people in his lifetime, it is surely unthinkable that he was able after his death to impress an alien like Moses, particularly when Moses lived, as Albright agrees, in the period of bitter reaction against Akhenaten.

Freud's chief reason for asserting that Moses was an Egyptian was his belief that Jewish monotheism was derived from "the monotheistic episode in Egyptian history" which is "the kernel of our thesis," and Moses, Freud argued, was the link between the two. Indeed as he imaginatively reconstructed the background, his hypothesis was

that Moses, a man of high rank and forceful in character, was an intimate follower
of Ikhnaton, who turned to the Israelites,
and attempted to preserve the Aton religion
through them and to make them express all
his religious ideals.

There is one difficulty in this hypothesis
which Freud had to recognize and it would
have daunted anyone less determined than
he: the religion of the Mosaic age did not
resemble the religion of the Ikhnaton
period as presented by Freud or indeed by
anyone else. As Freud himself put it:

These modern historians, well represented by
E. Meyer, follow the Biblical text in one decisive point. They concur that the Jewish
tribes, who later on became the people of
Israel, at a certain time accepted a new religion. But this event did not take place in
Egypt nor at the foot of a mount in the Sinai
peninsula, but in a place called Meribat-
Qadeš, an oasis distinguished by its abundance of springs and wells in the country
south of Palestine between the eastern end
of the Sinai peninsula and the western end
of Arabia. There they took over the worship of
a god Jahve, probably from the Arabic tribe
of Midianites who lived near by. Presumably
other neighbouring tribes were also followers
of that god.

This Jahve, Freud said, "was certainly a
volcano god." The particular mountain may
have been Sinai-Horeb which was believed
to be Jahve's abode, and Freud, following
Meyer, concluded that the original character of this god was that of "an uncanny,
bloodthirsty demon who walks by night and
shuns the light of day." Most critics nowa-
days, as we shall see, do not give to Yahweh
the character ascribed to him by Freud and
the authorities whom he follows, but there
is a common agreement that the religion of
Yahweh cannot be associated with the Aton
religion. Freud continued: "The mediator
between the people and the god at this birth
of a new religion was called Moses. He
was the son-in-law of the Midianite priest
Jethro and was tending his flocks when he
received the divine summons. Jethro visited

him in Qadeš to give him instructions." It
is small wonder that he added: "Our Egyptian Moses differs perhaps no less from the
Midian Moses than the universal god Aton
differed from the demon Jahve on his divine mountain. And if we concede any
measure of truth to the information fur-
nished by modern historians, then we have
to admit that the thread we wished to draw
from the surmise that Moses was an Egyptian has broken off for the second time;
this time, so it seems, without any hope of
its being tied again."

He nevertheless believed that in spite of
what the Biblical records had said, and all
the information produced by modern historians, he had succeeded in tying the required knot. To do it, however, he had to
produce two novel hypotheses: the first was
that there was an Egyptian Moses who
taught the Israelites the religion of Aton
and a second Moses who lived sixty to a
hundred years later who was the Midianite
Moses and who gave the Israelites the
Yahweh religion. There is not the slightest
evidence for a second Moses and no one
but Freud has ever suggested that there
were two. He, however, thought that the
suggestion made by Sellin in 1922 that
Moses met a violent end in a rebellion of
his stubborn and refractory people provided
a way out of this difficulty. But Sellin
thought that such a deed would have been
carried out in Shittim in the land east of
the Jordan and this will not do, for "we
shall see, however, that the choice of this
locality does not accord with our argument."
So Freud adopted the suggestion that a
Moses was killed by the Jews and that he
was the Egyptian Moses. As for the rest
"we venture to be independent of the historians in other respects and to blaze our
own trail." This he undoubtedly did. As
the book proceeded the trail became a
firmly established main road and the suggestion of Sellin became an unshakable
fact, so that on p. 98 we read: "Out of the
darkness which the Biblical Text has here
left — or rather created — the historical research of our days can distinguish two facts.

The first, discovered by E. Sellin, is that the Jews, who even according to the Bible were stubborn and unruly towards their lawgiver and leader, rebelled at last, killed him and threw off the imposed Aton religion as the Egyptians had done before them." Yet on p. 59 Freud had said: "Naturally I am not in a position to decide whether Sellin has correctly interpreted the relevant passages in the prophets. If he is right, however, we may regard as historically credible the tradition he recognized: for such things are not readily invented — there is no tangible motive for doing so." And the tradition to which he was referring was that of the murder of Moses. This despite the fact that Sellin himself had given up this suggestion as being completely untenable, even before Freud had written *Moses and Monotheism*. There is no other basis for believing in the existence of more than one Moses, and the fact that Freud believed it is surely one of the clearest examples of wish-fulfilment to be found anywhere.

There is, moreover, the further, apparently insuperable, difficulty that no trace of the teaching of an Egyptian Moses, a follower of Aton, can be found during the Mosaic age. A pure monotheism was only established among the Hebrews hundreds of years later and owed much to the efforts of the prophets. Freud now produced his second hypothesis: the Egyptian Moses taught the Israelites the monotheistic religion of the great reformer Aton, but after he had been killed all this teaching was repressed and did not emerge until about 500 years later. There is not the slightest proof of this, and the hypothesis was produced because without it Freud could not possibly maintain his main thesis of the relation between an Egyptian and a Hebrew monotheism. It is a fantastic hypothesis, and as Freud returned to it in the last section of his book under the title of "The Return of the Repressed" we shall deal with it later in this chapter.

If the date of the Exodus were known we could judge whether or not there was any possibility of the Ikhnaton period influencing Moses. Unfortunately, the dates of the Exodus and therefore of Moses are not so simply decided as even so profound a scholar as Meek thought they could be. Many of the leading authorities are hopelessly divided on the date of the Exodus. Professor S. A. Cook, Regius Professor of Hebrew in the University of Cambridge, in *The Old Testament. A Re-interpretation* (1936) provides a chronological summary in which he gives the date for Ikhnaton's reign as 1380–1362. The computed date of the Exodus he puts as 1447 B.C. If this were correct, then the age of Moses was considerably before Ikhnaton and there could be no question of the latter influencing the Mosaic age.

Albright, however, gives weighty evidence for placing the Exodus about the year 1290 B.C. and bases this date on the discovery made in 1937 in the remains of the latest Canaanite Lachish of a hieratic inscription dated to the year 1231 B.C. and possibly somewhat later, but in any case not earlier. This proves that the town fell into Israelite hands in or after that year. The Israel stele of Merneptah which is dated 1229 B.C. proved that Israel was already in western Palestine in force but had not yet settled down. If a generation of forty years be allowed for a Wilderness period we arrive at a date not later than about 1260 B.C. for the Exodus. Probably, however, a generation should be allowed for the occupation of eastern Palestine and the advance westwards in force, so this would bring the date to about 1290 B.C. Ikhnaton became Pharaoh in 1377 B.C. and reigned for seventeen years and so to about 1363 or 1360 B.C. If we accept this chronology then it is impossible that Moses could have been influenced directly by Ikhnaton.

In the Summary of Dates given as an appendix by Rowley in his *From Joseph to Joshua* the date of the Exodus is thirty years later than the one given by Albright:

circa 1370 B.C. Joseph taken into Egypt in reign of Ikhnaton, under whom he takes high office.

circa 1360 B.C. Descent into Egypt of Hebrews, particularly some of those who had failed to hold Shechem.

circa 1300 B.C. Oppression under Rameses II. Hebrews set to build Pithom and Rameses.

circa 1290 B.C. Moses born.

circa 1260 B.C. Exodus from Egypt under Moses.

Meek in his *Hebrew Origins* places the Exodus much later still: "For the enslaved Hebrews in Egypt a deliverer arose in course of time in the person of Moses, who took advantage of the chaotic state of affairs that developed in Egypt after the death of Seti II (*circa* 1215 B.C.) to lead his people out, or such of them as could or would follow him."

None of these chronologies, all of which are the work of the most distinguished scholars in this field, would make it possible for Moses to be what Freud suggested he was: an adherent of Ikhnaton himself. In themselves, Cook's and also Albright's dates would rule out any possible influence. The other dates for the Exodus are so much after the time of Ikhnaton that, in view of the violent reaction against Ikhnaton and all that he stood for, it is extremely difficult to believe that Moses could have come under his influence.

If Freud were correct in his main contentions we should expect to find some traces at least of the Aton religion during the Mosaic age. It is right, therefore, to consider the nature of Hebrew religion immediately following the Exodus. What, then, do we find in the Mosaic age? The Israelites believed that Yahweh was their God in a very special sense and, following the leadership of Moses, they believed themselves united with him in a solemn covenant so that they became his "peculiar people." They recognized that other nations had their own gods but as far as they were concerned Yahweh alone was to be worshipped. This is not to say that the whole of the nation was always undeviatingly faithful, for at times some of them forsook Yahweh and worshipped the local gods or baalim. But there was always a nucleus who remained faithful to Yahweh.

The anthropomorphic character of Yahweh is very deeply rooted in the Mosaic religion, and in fact he is far more anthropomorphic than the gods we find among the Egyptians or the Mesopotamians. Yahweh is sometimes referred to in a way which suggests that he has a human form although this is usually hidden by his glory. In Exodus xxxiii, 23 Moses is granted the supreme privilege of seeing the back of Yahweh but not the face, because "shall no man see Me and live." He was like his people and so could show love and hatred, joy and sorrow and even revenge and remorse although on a lofty plane. But he stood alone without a consort, or indeed family connections of any kind. In all this we are in a different atmosphere from the surrounding forms of religion. For instance the sun had no significant part to play at all. Yahweh is an anthropomorphic Supreme Being and not a solar or nature deity like Murduk, Amon-Re or Aton. Aton could be represented by a solar disc from which human hands emanated, whereas there was no physical representation of Yahweh whatsoever. There was nothing remote about him for he was interested in everything his people did, and Israel recognized Yahweh less and less as a Supreme Being or High God and more as a God who was first interested in them as individuals and as a nation, and so in their history, and finally in the history of the whole world.

Yahweh was not restricted to any special place. He was lord of all the cosmic forces and controlled the sun, the moon and the storm, but at the same time he was not identified with any of them. He dwelt in Heaven but could come down to a lofty mountain like Sinai, or to a shrine like the Tabernacle or to any place he might choose.

The tradition representing Moses as a lawgiver is so strong that probably the basis at least of such a statement as the Ten Commandments does go back to the movement associated with his name. It is unlikely to be earlier, and if with Meek and other Semitic scholars we accept them as being at least in general agreement with the movement which bears the name of Moses, we can see the force of the point which Meek makes in referring to the first commandment: "However the most we can claim for Moses in it is monolatry."

During the middle of the eighth century B.C. there arose a group of men, the prophets, who purified the traditional religion and taught a conception of God which was undoubtedly pure monotheism and of a remarkable kind. Not only was God one but he was perfectly good and he demanded goodness from his followers. The teaching about Yahweh during this age is summed up by T. H. Robinson in *The Teachers' Commentary*.

(*a*) Yahweh is Law. He was no capricious being like the gods of most nations but was consistent in all His actions.

(*b*) Yahweh is Lord of Nature. He was God of Creation and there was no other God responsible for any part of nature.

(*c*) Yahweh is Lord of History. He was no longer a tribal God but controlled the whole political world.

(*d*) Yahweh is the Lord of the end of things. At the end of all things Yahweh would vindicate, not Israel against other nations, but the principles of righteousness against Israel as His character required.

(*e*) Yahweh is Lord of Universal Morality. His interest in human conduct did not spring merely from the pride of a god who had laid down certain commands on a particular people but He watched over the actions of men everywhere and His Laws were valid for all nations whether they knew it or not for they were based on the nature of personality.

(*f*) Yahweh makes no ritual demands. It is righteousness He asks, not sacrifice, and it is hopeless to offer the latter as a substitute for the former.

(*g*) Yahweh is, in a special sense, the God of Israel. Although He is the Lord of the whole world, yet He has chosen Israel for His own purposes. She has then special privileges but also special responsibilities and if she fails to meet them she will receive special punishment.

This is monotheism but it is not the religion of Aton. Freud believed that it was nothing more than the emergence of the repressed from the racial unconscious. Yet surely the great prophets had something vital to do in the formulation of this unique conception of God. It was influenced by the past history of Israel and expressed the spirit of that nation. The prophets were great individualists and each emphasized the particular aspect of the general teaching which appealed most strongly to him. Hosea, speaking from the deep experiences of his own married life, spoke of love. Amos insisted on justice, on fair dealing between man and man. Isaiah's message was concerned with holiness and the importance of complete consecration on the part of Israel to Yahweh in recognition of the consecration and holiness of Yahweh towards Israel. The message is the expression of the prophet, and the prophet, although influenced by the nation, was an individual with his own particular utterance. As he himself recognized, he was responsible for the message he had to proclaim and was no mere sounding-board delivering a strange teaching from the depths of a racial unconscious which, all unknown to him, came through a first unknown Moses, from the reformer Ikhnaton.

The authors of *Before Philosophy* came to the definite conclusion that the religious thought of the Hebrews belonged to an entirely different atmosphere from that of Egypt and Mesopotamia. This book is of importance because in it a group of competent scholars survey the whole background with which *Moses and Monotheism* deals. In a final chapter on "The Emancipation of Thought from Myth" Professor and Mrs. Frankfort insist on the overwhelming distinction between Egyptian and Mesopotamian thought and belief and that of the Hebrews, and use as an illustration the Hebrew teaching about Yahweh:

The Hebrews arrived late upon the scene and settled in a country pervaded by influences from the two superior adjacent cultures. One would expect the newcomers to have assimilated alien modes of thought, since these were supported by such vast prestige. Untold immigrants from deserts and mountains had done so in the past; and many individual Hebrews did, in fact, conform to the ways of the Gentiles. But assimilation was not characteristic for Hebrew thought. On the contrary, it held out with a peculiar stubbornness and insolence against the wisdom of Israel's neighbours. It is possible to detect the reflection of Egyptian and Mesopotamian beliefs in many episodes of the Old Testament; but the overwhelming impression left by that document is one, not of derivation, but of originality.

Meek came to a similar conclusion: "It is one of the enigmas of history that the Hebrews were so little affected by the religion of Egypt, when both history and archaeology show such intimate contacts between the two."

Man is seldom a complete innovator in anything important and usually less so in religion than elsewhere. If Egypt was not the spiritual home of the religion of the Mosaic age where is that to be found?

One of the most interesting views, which admittedly is not shared by all scholars, is that the name of Yahweh and certain features of the Mosaic teaching about religion were derived from the Kenites, who were a nomadic tribe of the south of Palestine closely associated with the Amalekites. This view is supported and discussed in Rowley's Schweich Lectures *From Joseph to Joshua*.

The Biblical record describes how Moses had to leave Egypt for fear that his murder of an Egyptian would be discovered. We know that he went down to Midian and there married a daughter of Jethro. Rowley advances the interesting suggestion that a Levite belonging to the Israelite group that went down into Egypt could have married a Kenite woman. The mother of Moses had a name which was compounded with the name Yahweh, and even if we judged by that alone it would look as if an ancestor of Moses on his mother's side had married a Kenite woman. This at any rate would explain why, when Moses fled from Egypt, he went to a Kenite settlement; he could have gone there because they were his mother's people, just as Jacob, when he fled from Esau, went to his mother's kindred. During the period that Moses spent in the household of Jethro he would have come into touch with the religion professed by the priest Jethro. Possibly during that time Moses experienced a deep religious conversion, and became convinced that this God about whom he had now learnt so much was the powerful God who would deliver his fellow-countrymen from their bondage in Egypt. So he returned to that country and led his people out, to the sacred mountain of Sinai. Those, therefore, whom he led would have a different background from his own — if we can rely on these conjectures — and so, according to their traditions, the worship of Yahweh began with the coming of Moses to deliver them and the acceptance of the solemn Covenant of Sinai. This theory would at any rate help to explain the religion of the Mosaic age without straining our credulity to the extent that Freud does.

As we know, the father-in-law of Moses is sometimes called Jethro, a priest of Midian, and sometimes Reuel, a priest of Midian. Elsewhere it is stated that Hobab, the son of Reuel, was a Kenite and thus it would appear that the father-in-law of Moses was a Kenite. We also know that when Moses led the Israelites out of Egypt he was met by his father-in-law who, after he had heard of the great deliverance wrought by Yahweh, cried: "Now I know that Yahweh is greater than all the gods" (Exod. xviii. 11). He it was who then offered sacrifice to God and, after he had given Moses advice, left. The sacrifice at which Jethro officiated for the elders of Israel must have been the sacrifice to the God Yahweh, and it is probable that this Yahweh was the God to whom Jethro was priest. We can only understand his joy at the evidence of Yahweh's great power if Yahweh were the God whom he already served. . . .

Repression is defined in a glossary at the end of *Moses and Monotheism* as "the keeping of unacceptable ideas from consciousness, i.e. in the 'unconscious.'" This process Freud found repeatedly in his analytical work, but in *Moses and Monotheism* he claimed that just as the individual represses so does the race or mass: "The masses, too, retain an impression of the past in unconscious memory traces." Further passages make clear exactly what Freud is claiming for the part of repression in the racial unconscious. "The murder of the Father was brought home to the Jews, for fate decreed that they should repeat it on the person of Moses, an eminent father substitute." "The murder of Moses was such a repetition, and later on the supposed judicial murder of Christ, so that these events move into the foreground as causative agents." Freud even goes so far as to include the ideas of former ages among the contents of the racial unconscious: ". . . the archaic heritage of mankind includes not only dispositions, but also ideational contents, memory-traces of the experiences of former generations."

What has been repressed in the racial unconscious can, so Freud claimed, return in the same way as it does with the individual neurosis, and he illustrated his theme by the material given in *Moses and Monotheism.*

We can classify what Freud treated as the return of the repressed in the following way:

1. The memory of the Great Crime — the killing of the primaeval father.
2. The primaeval experience in the human family where in the return of the repressed the figure of the father, grown still more gigantic than even early experience in childhood made him, is given the status of a deity.
3. Such ideational material as the teaching by an Egyptian Moses of the monotheism which he had derived from Ikhnaton.

Freud repeated in *Moses and Monotheism* the theme of the slaying of the primal father of the horde and his belief that the knowledge of this crime remains in the racial unconscious and creates a continuing sense of guilt: ". . . I have no qualms in saying that men have always known — in this particular way — that once

upon a time they had a primaeval father and killed him." The memory and the guilt were always there, ready to return just like an outbreak of neurosis in the individual. Freud seized the briefly-held hypothesis of Sellin that the Israelites had killed the father of their race, Moses, and this murder he maintained was a repetition of the killing of the primal father. It made the Great Crime real to the race, and while remaining deeply buried in the racial unconscious increased the sense of guilt which continued to haunt the Israelites. . . .

Freud also believed that Moses, in teaching his followers about the one God, was not giving them a new idea "for it meant the re-animation of primaeval experience in the human family that had long ago faded from the conscious memory of mankind." He believed that the Father loomed as a gigantic figure in primaeval times and, raised to the status of a deity in the racial unconscious, returned to the memory of mankind.

This view of the powers of the racial unconscious is a highly original one, and so much is built on it that it merits careful examination. Ordinarily we think of repression as being a very individual affair and we do not expect what has been repressed in one person to emerge from someone else. It is surprising to claim that ideational contents are carried in a racial unconscious for hundreds of years. And as Freud admits: "This state of affairs is made more difficult, it is true, by the present attitude of biological science which rejects the idea of acquired qualities being transmitted to descendants. I admit, in all modesty, that in spite of this I cannot picture biological development proceeding without taking this factor into account." There is admittedly a process of repression relating to individuals and possibly a collective unconscious which preserves, as Jung maintains, important racial experiences which are stamped in over endless years and function in a form similar to what we mean by instincts. But nothing is known of any process which would preserve the speculative ideas of Ikhnaton on monotheism and religion through Moses in the unconscious of another nation for hundreds of years. It is surely more credible to believe that the thought and experience of such prophets as Amos,. Hosea, Isaiah and Jeremiah played some part, and that not a minor one, in the establishment of ethical monotheism among the Hebrews. If Ikhnaton had his vision, that is no reason why the great eighth-century prophets should not have had theirs.

Freud's argument that monotheistic teaching was latent for hundreds of years was a dangerous one for him to use, especially when he went on to claim that Ikhnaton was the first monotheist in history. According to his contention about the nature of the unconscious, we have no right to assume this, for monotheism might have remained latent in the unconscious of the Egyptian nation for hundreds of years to emerge during the Eighteenth Dynasty. There might have been monotheistic teaching among the Hyksos who invaded Egypt long before Ikhnaton and if, as some maintain, the Hyksos were Semites, all kinds of interesting possibilities would arise. Moreover those who, like Schmidt, argue for a universal primitive monotheism could explain by means of this theory how it had been repressed at various periods. Freud's hypothesis could be used in many directions if it could be accepted, but it cannot, and all the vast structure which he built on it was falsely based: consequently most of his arguments about the nature and contents of religious belief put forward in *Moses and Monotheism* and also in some of his other works have no weight. That, we believe, is the correct conclusion.

There are two aspects to Freud's theories about the rôle of Moses in the racial unconscious. One is that he is a father imago: "Without doubt it must have been a tremendous father imago that stooped in the person of Moses to tell the poor Jewish labourers that they were his dear children." Moses reanimated the primaeval experience in the human family and as a father imago helped to raise this to the status of deity. His other rôle was to pass on the teachings of Ikhnaton which then remained latent for so long, together with memories of the slaying of Moses.

There is, however, one flaw in Freud's argument that Moses reanimated the experience of the primaeval family situation and the slaying of the primal father. He stated that the first Moses was not the Father of Israel, but an idealistic Egyptian who determined to continue the Aton religion through the foreign Israelites. His motives were propagandist and so he was not a good substitute for the primal father. But the whole point of the argument in *Totem and Taboo,* repeated in *Moses and Monotheism,* was that the father of the horde was killed not because he was an aggressive and dominating figure, but through sexual jealousy: "All females were his property, the wives and daughters in his own horde as well as perhaps also those robbed from other hordes. The fate of the sons was a hard one; if they excited the father's jealousy they were killed or castrated or driven out." After they revolted and killed him they realized the futility of killing each other to obtain the succession which they desired, so "Each renounced the ideal of gaining for himself the position of father, of possessing his mother or sister. With this the taboo of incest and the law of exogamy came into being." There is not the slightest reason anywhere to think that anyone could even have wished to murder Moses through motives of this kind.

If God is nothing but "an exalted father," a projection from the primaeval family situation, and Moses merely another example of him and a return of this repressed material, what is the point of the elaborate theory that it was Ikhnaton who first produced the speculation of monotheism, which then spread through an Egyptian Moses, remaining latent in the racial unconscious until it was made active once more in the eighth century? Freud was trying to explain the emergence of monotheism through his concept of the racial unconscious in two ways, one through an experience of the primaeval family, common to the whole human race, and the other through the retaining by the racial unconscious of the ideational contents transmitted through Moses. If the former were operative, monotheism would arise everywhere. The latter would be unnecessary and surely could not be separately recognized.

What Freud had to say about the place of Jesus Christ and Paul does not fit well into the structure of *Moses and Monotheism*, although he tried to make it do so. According to Freud Moses came from Egypt with his new teaching, and was killed, later becoming a tremendous father imago. Approximately 1,300 or 1,400 years after his death a Jew was killed, a son of the nation, to atone for the deed of his brothers in killing Moses, and through him repeating the Great Crime. In actual fact He did not save His brothers from their guilt for most of them did not accept Him

as their Saviour. He was accepted as Saviour by the Gentiles, although there could be no question of their racial unconscious being burdened with the guilt of killing Moses.

All this may appear to fit in perfectly with the requirements of psychoanalytical reasoning. Yet it might appear to those who are accustomed to use other modes of reasoning as well, that it had been made to fit in too neatly. Since the time when Freud put forward the obscure hypothesis of the slaying of the primal father, ethnologists have described it as nonsense. Freud knew this, and even admitted it in *Moses and Monotheism*, but answered that he preferred to hold on to his own version. Facts of history, sound anthropology, convincing psychology in relation to the racial unconscious, evidence worthy of serious consideration or even solid argument — none of these is prominent in *Moses and Monotheism*.

Freud as Philosopher of History

BRUCE MAZLISH

Born in New York City in 1923, Bruce Mazlish studied history at Columbia University. After teaching at the University of Maine and at Columbia, Dr. Mazlish joined the faculty of the Massachusetts Institute of Technology in 1950. Author of several works, he is also coauthor with his M. I. T. colleague, J. Bronowski, of *The Western Intellectual Tradition: From Leonardo to Hegel* (New York, 1960).

IT MAY SURPRISE some readers to see Freud described as the last of the great classical philosophers of history. Yet, the description is an accurate one. The founder of psychoanalysis is in the tradition of Comte and Hegel, and especially of Vico, whose fulfillment he can well be considered. Like the latter, Freud worked out a

From pp. 381–382, 390–393, 394, 395–397, 400–403, and 404–405, in *The Riddle of History* by Bruce Mazlish. Copyright © 1966 by Harper & Row, Publishers. Reprinted by permission of Harper & Row, Publishers.

new science — in this case, psychoanalysis instead of philology — which offered important clues for solving the riddle of man's past.

In his initial work, of course, Freud concerned himself mainly with the individual's past, and he studied his subject in the office and the clinic rather than in the historical world. Focusing on unconscious mental processes, hitherto neglected or misunderstood, he discovered new methods and devised a whole range of new theories to explore the unplumbed depths of his patient's character. The result was a novel and startling view of individual man.

Then, boldly, Freud extrapolated his psychoanalytic findings to men in general and to the collective past. As part of this effort, he envisioned a new genesis, or origin, of man as a cultural animal, and then traced the path of humanity through time. He concerned himself with such topics as the psychological roots of religion and morality, the direction of history, and the means by which that direction is pursued. He analyzed the actors in the historical drama, both the hero and the masses who follow him, and attempted to work out a group psychology as earlier he had labored at an individual psychology. Lastly, as he had analyzed individual neuroses in his clinical experience, so he tried to analyze the neuroses of the group in historical experience. The only cure for the latter (as for the former), according to Freud, is consciousness of the hitherto unconscious past. Thus, in his new version of an old subject, philosophy of history becomes both a diagnosis and a therapy for the ills of mankind.

* * *

At the very entrance to Freud's historical world, it is well to consider briefly the nature of his recital. The model for Freud's work in the area of culture is the "case history," but now macroscopic in its use. His approach to the origins of the group neurosis known as history is still clinical, and he writes up his reports as if he were dealing with an individual patient, only of larger dimensions. All of Freud's theories in philosophy of history are thus "grounded," to use an energy metaphor, in his observations of living subjects and in the method by which he writes up these findings.

The case history itself, however, is a somewhat suspect scientific document. As Freud remarked about one of his earliest reported accounts, in the *Studies in Hysteria,* "I still find it a very strange thing that the case histories I describe read like short stories and lack, so to speak, the serious imprint of science." His opponents were equally quick to make this comment, as when Krafft-Ebing, chairman of the session of the Society of Psychiatry and Neurology in Vienna listening to the paper on "The Etiology of Hysteria" (1896), remarked dryly: "It sounds like a scientific fairy tale." For himself, Freud produced the consoling thought that "it is obviously the nature of the material itself that is responsible for this [the short story aspect] rather than my own choice."

So, too, *Totem and Taboo* was labeled by one reviewer, an anthropologist, as a *Just So* story. While apropos in the sense that Freud was a great admirer of Kipling's tales, this remark once again seeks to dismiss Freud's work as largely a fairy tale.

Now, in a strange way, these criticisms inadvertently point to the crucial feature of Freud's case histories; yet they miss the essential point. Freud's concern is with "fairy tales," but with their *analysis* and not with their mere *recital.* Clearly, this is not to say that Freud's analysis in a particular case is always correct; that remains for further discussion. It is to say that in external appearance his reports look suspiciously like short stories or fairy tales, without thereby being such. Instead, these "short story" reports are intended to be sober, scientific case studies of cultural events.

There is another, similar ambiguity involved in Freud's use of what he called "scientific myths." On one level, these are merely hypotheses or useful fictions, heuristic devices to allow for a provisional ordering of the data. Thus, as he wrote to Albert Einstein, "Does not every science come in the end to a kind of mythology?" On another level, however, myths in their primitive form are perhaps the earliest means of scientific cognition of *actual events,* and to be taken seriously as such. And on a third level, they merely represent psychic, but not historical, reality. Freud wavered among these definitions, and seemed unconscionably undisturbed about using them so loosely.

The difficulty is compounded, however, because Freud was not only *constructing* a scientific myth but presumably *analyzing* historical myths. We see the confusion illustrated in his comments in *Group Psychology and the Analysis of the Ego.* There, starting with the "scientific myth of the father of the primal horde," his own construction, he then passes immediately, as part of his hypothesis or scientific myth, to the historical development of the heroic myth. Thus, Freud supposes that after the murder of the father by the brothers grouped together, "some individual in the exigency of his longing, may have been moved to free himself from the group and take over the father's part. He who did this was the first epic poet; and the advance was achieved in his imagination. This poet disguised the truth with lies in accordance with his longing. He invented the heroic myth." Methodologically, of course, Freud's *analysis* of the heroic myth must come first, and lead him next to the *construction* of his own scientific myth, which is then to be checked against further data of all sorts. As Freud presents his work, however, the reader is made to move the other way, and he does so with the awkward feeling that, in fact, it is the way Freud himself moved. Ambiguity, so close to Freud's heart, has here led close to incomprehensibility.

Now, however, it is time to enter into the details of Freud's historical account. We shall then see, in action, his employment of the case study and the scientific myth, and judge how useful and valid is his novel approach.

In a postscript, written when he was 79,

to his *Autobiography,* Freud made the following revealing, although perhaps slightly misleading, statement:

My interest, after making a lifelong *détour* through the natural sciences, medicine and psychotherapy, returned to the cultural problems which had fascinated me long before, when I was a youth scarcely old enough for thinking. At the very climax of my psychoanalytic work, in 1912, I had already attempted in *Totem and Taboo* to make use of the newly discovered findings of analysis in order to investigate the origins of religion and morality. I now carried this work further in two later essays, *The Future of an Illusion* (1927), and *Civilization and Its Discontents* (1930). I perceived ever more clearly that the *events of human history,* the interactions between human nature, cultural development and the precipitates of primaeval experiences (the most prominent example of which is religion) *are no more than a reflection* of the dynamic conflicts between the ego, the id, and the superego, which psychoanalysis studies in the individual — are the very same processes repeated upon a wider stage [italics added].

In pursuit of his cultural interests, besides the books mentioned, Freud completed at the very end of his life *Moses and Monotheism. . . .*

The key motif or, better, "scientific myth" for *Totem* came from Charles Darwin. "In 1912," Freud tells us, "I took up a conjecture of Darwin's to the effect that the primitive form of human society was that of a horde ruled over despotically by a powerful male. I attempted to show that the fortunes of this horde have left indestructible traces upon the history of human descent; and, especially, that the development of totemism, which comprises in itself the beginnings of religion, morality, and social organization, is concerned with the killing of the chief by violence and the transformation of the paternal horde into a community of brothers." If we look at this passage closely, remembering too Freud's youthful enthusiasm for Darwin's theories, we can confidently put forward the suggestion that Freud, in *Totem,* saw himself as, first, completing Darwin's evolutionary account of the "descent" of the human species from its primal animal form, and, second, tracing the resulting "origin" of human society. We can see now that Freud was seeking to understand *in a scientific way* the genesis of man as a cultural animal, using the science of psychoanalysis as the lens by which to study his chosen species' evolution. . . .

We have already had a brief synopsis of what Freud's instinct led him to. He himself repeated his "Just So" story a number of times, and gives an especially useful précis, which shows us how he used his borrowed material, in *Moses and Monotheism*. There he tells us that in *Totem* he made use of

. . . certain theoretical reflections of Charles Darwin, J. J. Atkinson, and especially Robertson Smith, and combined them with findings and suggestions from psychoanalytic practice. From Darwin I borrowed the hypothesis that men originally lived in small hordes; each of the hordes stood under the rule of an older male, who governed by brute force, appropriated all the females, and belaboured or killed all the young males, including his own sons. From Atkinson I received the suggestion that this patriarchal system came to an end through a rebellion of the sons, who united against the father, overpowered him, and together consumed his body. Following Robertson Smith's totem theory, I suggested that this horde, previously ruled by the father, was followed by a totemistic brother clan. In order to be able to live in peace with one another the victorious brothers renounced the women for whose sake they had killed the father, and agreed to practise exogamy. The power of the father was broken and the families were regulated by matriarchy. The ambivalence of the sons towards the father remained in force during the whole further development. Instead of the father a certain animal was declared the totem; it stood for their ancestor and protecting spirit, and no one was allowed to hurt or kill it. Once a year, however, the whole clan assembled for a feast at which the otherwise revered totem was torn to pieces and eaten. No one was permitted to abstain from this feast; it was the solemn repetition of the father-murder, in which social order, moral laws, and religion had had their beginnings.

Did Freud really believe in the murder of the primal father as an actual event? First of all, when challenged, he retorted, "I am not an ethnologist, but a psychoanalyst. It was my good right to select from ethnological data what would serve me for my analytic work." Next, his thesis is watered down a bit by the admission that "the story is told in a very condensed way, as if what in reality took centuries to achieve, and during that long time was repeated innumerably, had happened only once." The real qualification occurs at the end of *Totem* itself. Discussing the overvaluation of their psychic acts by primitives, Freud posits that "Accordingly the mere hostile *impulse* against the father, the mere existence of a wishful *phantasy* of killing and devouring him would have been enough to produce the moral reaction that created totemism and taboo. . . . No damage would thus be done to the causal chain stretching from the beginning to the present day, for psychical reality would be strong enough to bear the weight of these consequences." Having conceded this much, however, Freud then retreats to his original position: "Primitive men . . . are uninhibited," he concludes, "thought passes directly into action. With them it is rather the deed that is a substitute for the thought. And that is why, *without laying claim to any finality of judgment*, I think that in the case before us it may safely be assumed that 'in the beginning was the Deed' [italics added]."

What shall we say to Freud's great myth? First, I must note that my précis has ignored the detail with which Freud pursues the stages of "causal connection," stretching from the beginning to the present time, however, this lacuna is permissible because the question of the original "deed" is independent of the later development (which, in any case, I shall treat later on). Second, I must point out that Freud, at least in principle, is perfectly in the right, as long as he does not distort or suppress ethno-logical data, in wishing to employ the touchstone of psychoanalysis on the ma-terials of anthropology. In that case, the judgment on the validity of his psycho-analytic findings must come from the clinic and not from the field and bush. Third, I must confess that my précis gives little ground for judging Freud's application of psychoanalysis to prehistory; I have not even touched on the wealth of illustrative and comparative materials (for example, the comparison of the compulsion involved in primitive taboos with the délire de toucher of individual psychotics, or the ambivalence centering around the totem worship with that animating everyday life), which is spread before us in Totem. The book must be read fully for these details.

* * *

I must be content here not to pass final judgment on the actual details of his theory in Totem and Taboo, but simply to invoke admiration for his pioneering attempt at finding psychological meaning in the hid-den "events" of the past. As Freud re-marked about his own efforts, we glimpse "a hypothesis which may seem fantastic but which offers the advantage of establishing an unsuspected correlation between groups of phenomena that have hitherto been dis-connected."

If Totem appears fantastic, Moses and Monotheism has seemed to most scholars even more so. The Moses book, however, is a natural development of the Totem hy-pothesis, continuing the story of man's cul-tural evolution from the totemic organiza-tion of society to the emergence of the monotheistic religions. Like Totem, it seeks to establish an "unexpected unity" and to do so by psychoanalytic hypotheses. A brilliant, exaggerated tour de force, filled with illuminations, it illustrates the specu-lative impulse, which Freud as a young man had "ruthlessly to check," springing too abruptly and detached from the em-pirical data. Yet, it is a serious and im-portant book, to be read with deep interest.

The work is rooted in Freud's lifelong involvement with the legendary Moses. As Ernest Jones remarks, "There is every rea-son to suppose that the grand figure of Moses himself, from Freud's early Biblical studies to the last book he ever wrote, was one of tremendous significance to him. Did he represent the formidable Father-Image or did Freud identify with him? Appar-ently both, at different periods." Thus, in 1912, the same year as he was writing Totem and Taboo, he began to compose an essay on the meaning of Michelangelo's Moses statue in Rome. Based on extended contemplation of the statue, for Freud had sat before it for hours, the essay "The Moses of Michelangelo" was finished in 1914. I shall single out only one point about this work. It is Freud's acute ability to observe details, such as that the tables in the statue were held upside down, and then to use these details in the construction of a psy-choanalytic interpretation. Basing himself on this observation, Freud opposes the general view that the statue represented Moses as about to rise and chastise his dis-obedient followers dancing around the Golden Calf. Instead, he interprets the statue as showing Moses, suddenly aware that the sacred tables are about to fall to the ground, restraining himself with a mighty effort.

The same attention to the small detail and then the construction upon it of a psy-chological analysis is manifested in Moses and Monotheism. Written over various periods, finished under the shadow of the Nazis in 1939, broken and uneven in style, the book is nevertheless a true example of Freud's method. It starts with sharp at-tention to a small detail, Moses' name, and proceeds from that along its "fantastic" path.

The opening thesis of the book is that Moses was an Egyptian, not a Jew. Freud reaches this conclusion on two grounds: (1) a philological investigation of the name, Moses; and (2) an analysis of Moses' birth and exposure in terms of other "birth of the hero" myths. Freud next postulates that Moses was a follower of Amenhotep IV, the Egyptian Pharaoh (c. 1375 B.C.) who changed his name to Ikhnaton and set up the worship of the one God, Aton. With the counterrevolution against Ikhnaton's monotheism by the priests of the old-style worship, Moses, according to Freud's account, seized on an unusual destiny. Rejected by his own people in Egypt, Moses "chose" the Jews (henceforth the "chosen" people of God), a barbarous, uncultured people, and, leading them out of bondage, shaped a "holy nation" out of them. Freud adds that Moses also introduced the Jews to the custom of circumcision, otherwise practised only by the Egyptians.

At this point, Freud pauses to hear the reproach "that I have built up this edifice of conjectures with too great a certainty, for which no adequate grounds are to be found in the material itself." Reminding the reader that he has already himself stressed the hypothetical, the heuristic, character of his investigation, Freud plunges on to his second major thesis. Basing himself on a "discovery" of the biblical scholar, Ernst Sellin, Freud surmises that the Jews, chafing under the Mosaic laws, murdered Moses, the father figure. This re-enactment of the primal horde experience was as traumatic as the first experience. Forgotten and repressed through a long latency period, the material was psychologically "remembered" by Moses' followers, the Levites, even after their merging with other Jewish tribes, the Midianites. Without following Freud's involved account of the relations of the two segments of the Jewish race, we come to his conclusion that, with the Israelitic prophets, the original Mosaic religion was restored.

The unraveling of this history, Freud tells us, has been made difficult because the texts have been transformed and distorted. "The distortion of a text," however, he points out, "is not unlike a murder." It leaves traces, and these we can decipher with the magnifying glass of psychoanalysis. Since the latter tells us with certainty that "religious phenomena are to be understood only on the model of the neurotic symptoms of the individual, which are so familiar to us, as a return of long-forgotten important happenings in the primeval history of the human family," we know exactly what to look for in mankind's history. The murder of Moses, recapitulating the primal crime, is the "long-forgotten important happening" which has generated the obsessional neurosis that has taken form as the Jewish religion. Totemism has been supplanted by monotheism. . . .

As with *Totem,* only more so, the *Moses* thesis is hard either to prove or to disprove. The events which it claims to explain are buried under the swirl of time, and there is little clear documentary evidence surviving. Some of Freud's subsidiary theories, such as the inheritance of acquired mental traits (a form of Lamarckian psychoanalysis, which we have not yet discussed), raise additional difficulties. Many of his "facts" are suspect: Moses' name may have been Egyptian, but the Jews, then as now, have frequently taken their names from the dominant culture in which they lived; the murder of Moses is dubious; and various of Freud's philological identifications are simply incorrect. We can only conclude, therefore, that Freud's application of psychoanalytic insights to the traditional accounts of the origins of the Jewish and Christian religions results merely in a tenuous connection with what is, to begin with, unsatisfactory empirical data. The *Moses* book is indeed a very speculative work in the philosophy of history. What remains from Freud's work here is a chain of great "ifs," and a number of ingenious suggestions.

V. THE HEBREW ORIGINS OF MONOTHEISM

Abraham and Moses

HARRY M. ORLINSKY

Born in Ontario, Canada in 1908, Harry M. Orlinsky taught at the Baltimore Hebrew College from 1936 to 1944. Since 1944 he has been a member
of the faculty at the Jewish Institute of Religion, Hebrew Union College, in
New York City. He served as editor-in-chief of the *New Translation of the
Holy Scriptures: The Torah.*

THE PATRIARCHAL CONCEPTION OF GOD AND THE COVENANT

SOME FEATURES in the patriarchal stage of Israelite history stand out with especial significance. While the picture in detail is still far from clear, the Biblical and the newer archaeological data combine to indicate that the patriarchs practiced a religion which, while not monotheistic in our sense of the term, was yet not polytheistic either.

Its basic concept, later to develop into national significance, was the "covenant." This was the tribal practice of entering into an agreement with one particular god, so that the deity would devote himself entirely to the covenanters, in return for their exclusive obedience and loyal trust. Abraham entered into a mutually exclusive agreement with God, "the God of Abraham," whereby Abraham was to recognize and worship no other deity and God was to protect and seek the welfare of Abraham and his family exclusively. In this regard, the Hebrews went far beyond their Mesopotamian counterparts, where the contractual relationship remained on a purely eco-

nomic *quid pro quo* basis and the magic element played a most important role.

When Isaac renewed Abraham's covenant, God became "the Kinsman of Isaac." For Jacob, God was "the Champion of Jacob." Abraham's brother, Nahor, the one left behind in Haran, likewise adopted a personal god. When Abraham's grandson Jacob and Nahor's grandson Laban settled a dispute between themselves, Jacob said to Laban, "If the God of my father, the God of Abraham and the Kinsman of Isaac, had not been with me, you would have sent me away empty" (Genesis 31:42). Whereupon Laban answered, "Let the God of Abraham and the God of Nahor, the God of their father, judge between us" (verse 53).

It would be going too far to attribute to the patriarchal Hebrews a belief in the existence of one and only one God. In a sense they may be said to have practiced — but without defining — monotheism. While they probably did not think of denying the existence of other gods, and some mighty ones among them at that, the patriarchs attached themselves to one God, and Him alone they worshiped. With Him, they en-

From Harry M. Orlinsky, *Ancient Israel*, 2nd ed. (Ithaca: 1960), pp. 21–23, 33–34. © 1960 by
Cornell University. Used by permission of Cornell University Press.

tered voluntarily into a covenant which was binding forever, never to be broken under penalty of severe punishment and, theoretically at least, even complete rejection. It is not possible to understand the subsequent career of Israel without understanding these two inseparable concepts which arose in patriarchal times: practical monotheism and the personal covenant between the patriarchal families and their God.

* * *

MOSES AND THE COVENANT

The Covenant between God and the new nation, a factor of fundamental importance in Israel's career, came into being during this period. The relationship between the patriarchs and their God had begun, according to the social patterns of seminomadic family life, as a personal arrangement. In Moses' first experience with the Deity, at the theophany in the burning bush (Exodus 3), the relationship was also personal; and in accord with the patriarchal tradition, the Deity Himself acquired a new personal name, YHWH, which is usually rendered "Lord" or "Jehovah." [1]

The experiences of the Exodus and the Wandering gradually forged the more individualistic elements into the new tribal or national unit. The purpose of the Exodus was not merely to free a group of slaves for their own sakes, but for something far greater in scope and significance, the creation of a new nation. The direct relationship between God and the Nation was the new element created by the forces of history and circumstance. From that point on, and throughout the entire Bible henceforth, the new Covenant, a national pact between God and His people, sealed by the act of the Exodus, replaced the older, individual covenants between God and the patriarchal leaders.

[1] The Hebrew term consists of four letters, YHWH, and hence is called the Tetragrammaton. Some time after about the fifth century B.C., the original pronunciation of the name ceased to be employed for ordinary purposes, and the term Adonai, "Lord," came to be substituted for it. The term Jehovah is a relatively recent creation (about fourteenth century A.D.), by a Christian who erroneously read the vowels of Adonai together with the consonants of YHWH. The Revised Standard Version (New York, 1952) follows the tradition of the King James (so-called Authorized) Version, the Revised Version, and the Jewish Publication Society Translation in rejecting the term Jehovah, usually in favor of LORD.

Many scholars believe that the original pronunciation of YHWH was Yahweh. The evidence for this belief, however, is not decisive, and there are also very considerable differences of opinion as to what the term meant originally.

Moses as Monotheist

WILLIAM FOXWELL ALBRIGHT

Born in Chile in 1891, William Foxwell Albright served as Director of the American School of Oriental Research in Jerusalem from 1920 to 1929 and from 1933 to 1936. He has engaged in numerous archaeological excavations in the Middle East. From 1929 until his retirement in 1958 he was W. W. Spence Professor of Semitic Languages at Johns Hopkins University. The author of *The Archaeology of Palestine*, he has also written many other books and articles.

WE ARE handicapped in dealing with this subject by the fact that all our literary sources are relatively late . . . and that we must therefore depend upon a tradition which was long transmitted orally. Many scholars go so far as to deny the historian any right to use these sources to determine what the religion of Moses actually was. Under the circumstances we must content ourselves with establishing certain facts and some other probabilities. In the first place, it is absurd to deny that Moses was actually the founder of the Israelite commonwealth and the framer of Israel's religious system. This fact is emphasized so unanimously by tradition that it may be regarded as absolutely certain. Nowhere is there the slightest breath of doubt cast on this irrefragable fact by Israelite tradition. If we regard Zoroaster, Buddha, and Confucius as the founders of nomistic religions we cannot deny this right to Moses. In this case we are no more justified in insisting that the religion introduced by Moses was radically different from that of the Book of Exodus than we should be in trying to divorce the other higher religions which we have named from their founders. The Pentateuch reflects a series of traditions coming from circles in which the "law of Moses" was the ultimate standard. In order to determine the details of this law there had to be priests or scribes whose primary function it was to preserve and transmit them. As has recently been pointed out by S. Gandz (1935), there was a class of priests who are called by Jeremiah (2:8) "holders of the law" (*tôfesê hattôrah*), with name and function which remind us of the Moslem "holders" (*ḥuffâz*) of the Qur'an. In many ways the transmission of the Torah must have resembled that of the Tradition (*ḥadîth*) in Islam; the apparent lack of the validating "chain" (*isnâd*) in Israel is presumably due to the anonymity of authors and scholars there (aside from the prophets of the eighth century and later). In the course of time a great many laws and practices which can hardly have been Mosaic were introduced into Israel; their lateness is often established by comparison of the forms which they assume in JE, D, and P, which show a progressive development first adequately emphasized by Wellhausen.

There is absolute unanimity in our sources about the name given his God by Moses. The spelling $YHWH$ (pronounced *Yahweh*, as we know from Greek transcriptions) is always found in prose pas-

From William Foxwell Albright, *From the Stone Age to Christianity*, 2nd ed. (Baltimore: 1946), pp. 196–207. Reprinted by permission of The Johns Hopkins University Press.

sages in the Hebrew Bible, as well as in the Mesha Stone (ninth century) and the Lachish Letters (cir. 589 B.C.). Beside this fuller form there was also a normally abbreviated form *Yahu* (the jussive form of the imperfect causative which appears in *Yahweh*), which is found in all early personal names (shortened in northern Israel to *-yau-* and after the Exile to *-yah*). It has often been maintained in the past thirty years that *Yahu* is more original than *Yahweh*, but all the epigraphic and linguistic facts are utterly opposed to this paradoxical view. It has also been insisted that this or that earlier non-Israelite divine name or element in a personal name shows the existence of the prototype of the Tetragrammaton before Moses. In itself this is not impossible, but every single suggestion has been effectively disproved, including the latest from Ugarit, where Virolleaud suggests that a word *yw* is identical with *Yahweh*. Unfortunately, the context does not lend itself in the least to such an interpretation, and the supposed *yw* should probably be read *yr*, "offspring," which suits the context well, so far as it is preserved. It is well known today that the most plausible of the older suggestions, Accadian *yaum* in the name *Yaum-ilu,* means simply "Mine (is the god)." Many different meanings have been attributed to *Yahweh* by scholars who recognized its relative antiquity, but only one yields any suitable sense: "He causes to be." The other suggestions, "He blows, He fells, He loves, He is kindly," etc., are totally without parallel in ancient Near-Eastern onomastics. It is objected that "to cause to be" is too abstract a meaning for so early a period. This again is erroneous, since Egyptian and Accadian texts of pre-Mosaic days swarm with illustrations of this idea, beginning with the Pyramid Texts. Linguistically the form *yahweh* can only be causative, and to judge from many analogies in Babylonia, Egypt, and Canaan, it is an abbreviation of a longer name or litanic formula. A few illustrations must suffice. In Sumerian Babylonia the name *Shagan* (later *Shakkan*), belonging to the god of animal husbandry, is an abbreviation of *Ama-shagan-gub,* "He who Assists Bearing Mothers"; *Dumuzi* (later *Tammuz*) stands for *Dumu-zid-abzu; Asari* (a name of Marduk) represents the fuller *Asari-lu-dug; Gish* stands for *Gishbilgamesh* (later *Gilgamesh*), etc. Similar abbreviated formulae are common as divine names in later Accadian and Egyptian religion: cf. Accadian *Aṣûshu-namer, Uṣuramatsa,* and Egyptian *Iusas,* etc. It is, indeed, probable that many Egyptian names of gods are just as abbreviated as the names of kings and commoners are known to be in all early periods; e.g., the name *Osiris* is probably an abbreviation of the fuller *Osiris-onnophris.* A most remarkable illustration comes from the Canaanite religion of the 15th century B.C., where the standing appellation of the storm-god, Baal, usually given as *Al'iyan,* appears in its full form as "I prevail (*'al'iyu*) over the champions whom I meet in the land of battle." The abbreviated name accordingly means simply "I will surely prevail." The enigmatic formula in Ex. 3:14, which in biblical Hebrew means "I am what I am," if transposed into the form in the third person required by the causative *Yahweh,* can only become *Yahweh asher yihweh* (later *yihyeh*), "He Causes to be what Comes into Existence." Later this formula was modified, presumably because the old causative was no longer used in later Hebrew. In the dialect of Moses the formula may even have been *Yahweh zê-yihweh,* employing the *zê* which appears as a relative preposition in Canaanite and poetic Hebrew as well as in the appellation of Yahweh in Jud. 5:5, *Zê-Sinai,* "the One of Sinai" (as first pointed out by H. Grimme, in accordance with widespread West-Semitic usage). If the restored formula were isolated one would be justified despite the evidence in suspecting its correctness, but we have it again and again in Egyptian texts of the second millennium B.C.: "(a god) who causes to be (or who creates) what comes into existence" (e.g., repeatedly in the great hymn to Amun from the 15th century B.C.). Even if this view should prove to be wrong, there is ample evidence in the Bible that the Israelites had always regarded Yahweh as Creator of All.

Another original characteristic of the Israelite God was that He stood alone, without any family connections, whether consort, son, or daughter. The nearest approach to attributing a family to Him that we meet before the Exile is the term *benê El* or *benê ha-'elôhîm*, "sons of God," employed for the angels, but this expression which was borrowed, as we shall see, from Canaanite does not necessarily have any more concrete meaning than does the frequent reference to the Israelites as children of God; both angels and Israelites were created by God and consequently might be poetically called His "children."

Still another equally original characteristic of Yahweh is that He is not restricted to any special abode. As the lord of all cosmic forces, controlling sun, moon, and storm but not identified with any of them, His normal dwelling-place is in heaven, from which He may come down, either to a lofty mountain like Sinai, to a shrine like the Tabernacle, or to any spot which He may choose. It is very significant that early Israelite poetry refers in only the most general terms to Mount Seir and Edom (Song of Deborah), to Teman and Mount Paran (the hymn imbedded in Habakkuk 3), to Sinai, Seir, and Paran (Deut. 33). The early Israelites laid so little stress on the exact spot that even the name of the mountain varies in our prose sources (Sinai or Horeb). This does not mean that it was not a sacred spot, but that there was no special cult associated with it, so the precise name and location were unimportant. The same situation is found in the early Christian church with reference to the location of the inn where Jesus was born and the tomb in which He was buried. The frequently stated view that Sinai must have been a volcano, a view popularized by A. Musil and Ed. Meyer, is without any solid basis. J. Morgenstern has effectively shown that the biblical theophany of Yahweh in

Ex. 19 must be explained through the Hebrew imagery connected with the Glory of Yahweh (*kebhôdh YHWH*). There is no volcano, active or extinct, in all Sinai or Midian proper. However, in adjacent regions of Hauran and Arabia there are many volcanoes which must have been active within the past few thousands of years. It is, therefore, quite possible that the sublime picture of the theophany in Exodus 19 was ultimately influenced by folk memories of volcanic eruptions (preserved in myth or metaphor), combined with more recent recollections of terrific thunder-storms in the mountains of northwestern Arabia or Syria. In other words, the sublime description of the theophany may owe certain features to the two most majestic spectacles vouchsafed to mankind: a sub-tropical thunder-storm and a volcanic eruption. We cannot emphasize too strongly that the principle of skeuomorphism . . . operates even more frequently in the world of ideas than it does in that of objects. Many ideas whose origin cannot be explained from the culture or the environment in which they are found, have been taken over from an entirely different cultural environment where they have a perfectly logical explanation.

Just as there is nothing in the Mosaic tradition which demands a derivation of Yahweh from an original volcanic deity or storm-god, so there is nothing which requires us to explain Him as a modified moon-god. It is improbable that the name *Sînai* is derived from that of Sumerian *Zen* (older *Zu-en*), Accadian *Sin*, the moon-god worshipped at Ur (in his form Nannar) and at Harran, since there is no indication that the name *Sin* was ever employed by the Canaanites or the Semitic nomads of Palestine. It is much more likely that the name *Sînai* is connected with the place-name *Sîn*, which belongs to a desert plain in Sinai as well as to a Canaanite city in Syria and perhaps to a city in the northeastern Delta of Egypt. It has also long been recognized that it may somehow be connected with *seneh* (Aram. *sanyâ*), the name of a kind of bush where Moses is said to have first witnessed the theophany of Yahweh. The usual aetiological explanation is inadequate, though possible.

Fundamental to early Israelite religion and profoundly rooted in Mosaic tradition is the anthropomorphic conception of Yahweh. Among the Egyptians, Mesopotamians, and Canaanites we find tendencies in this direction, but the concept of deity remained fluid and subject to extraordinary variation. Without considering the primitive dynamistic and corporative elements inherent in the concept of deity in the ancient Near East, we have only to glance at the mythologies, the iconographies, and the litanies to see that Near-Eastern gods shifted in disconcerting fashion from astral form to zoomorphic, dendromorphic, and composite manifestations. Yahweh, on the other hand, is virtually always referred to in the earlier sources in a way which suggests His human form though His body was usually hidden in a refulgent envelope called His Glory (kabhôdh). The most drastic and at the same time the clearest and presumably the most archaic illustration is the passage Ex. 33:23, where by special grace Moses sees Yahweh's back but not His face, "for there shall no man see Me and live." In the same way He appears in the early sources as having traits of human psychology, such as capacity for love and hatred, joy and sorrow, revenge and remorse, though always on a heroic plane.

There has been a great deal of futile writing about the anthropomorphism of early Israel. First of all, we must be very cautious in using material from the stories of Genesis 1–11, since most of this goes back to the Patriarchal Age, sometimes perhaps in its very wording (e.g., Gen. 6:1–4). To be sure, some of these stories are more recent and they have nearly all been more or less influenced by later monotheistic conceptions (so for example in the Story of the Flood when compared with the cuneiform version). Similarly, we must be careful not to make uncritical deductions as to Mosaic or later Israelite religion from

the narratives of the Patriarchs (Gen. 12–50), most of which come down, as we have seen, in substantially their present form from pre-Mosaic days. Thus the appearances of God in Gen. 18–19 are to be explained from pre-Mosaic polytheism, though the narratives have been revised in such a way as not to offend later Israelite, or for that matter Jewish or Christian readers.

Secondly, it cannot be emphasized too strongly that the anthropomorphic conception of Yahweh was absolutely necessary if the God of Israel was to remain a God of the individual Israelite as well as of the people as a whole. For the limited few who are natural mystics or have learned to employ certain methods to attain ecstatic state, the theological concepts attached to deity matter relatively little; there is a striking parallelism between the psychology of mysticism in Judaism, Islam, Buddhism, and Christianity. For the average worshipper, however, it is very essential that his god be a divinity who can sympathize with his human feelings and emotions, a being whom he can love and fear alternately, and to whom he can transfer the holiest emotions connected with memories of father and mother and friend. In other words, it was precisely the anthropomorphism of Yahweh which was essential to the initial success of Israel's religion. Like man at his noblest the God of Israel might be in form and affective reactions, but there were in Him none of the human frailties that make the Olympian deities of Greece such charming poetic figures and such unedifying examples. All the human characteristics of Israel's deity were exalted; they were projected against a cosmic screen and they served to interpret the cosmic process as the expression of God's creative word and eternally active will.

Equally vital to Mosaic religion was the aniconic character of Yahweh, who could not be represented in any visual or tangible form. In spite of the unanimous testimony of Israelite tradition, scholars have made repeated efforts to prove the existence of representations of deity in early Israel. Every effort of this kind has been based on subjective arguments and on arbitrary assumptions which have won only the most limited acceptance even in friendly circles. Of course, it would be equally unscholarly to deny the *possibility* of such images or portrayals in material form. But the testimony of our written sources, plus the completely negative results of excavation, should be evidence enough to prove that Yahwism was essentially aniconic and that material representations were foreign to its spirit from the beginning. We shall show below that there is no basis whatever for the idea that Yahweh was worshipped in bull form by the northern tribes at Bethel and Dan. The golden calf simply formed the pedestal on which the invisible Yahweh stood, just as in the Temple of Solomon the invisible Glory of God was enthroned above the cherubim; conceptually the two ideas are virtually identical.

After the demonstration by R. Hartmann and especially by H. Lammens of nomadic Arab parallels to the portable Tabernacle and Ark of the Covenant, some of them going far back into pre-Islamic times, it is captious to refuse them Mosaic date, since they were completely foreign to sedentary Canaanite practice and since they are known to have persisted for some time after the Conquest of Palestine. The archaeologist no longer has any difficulty in proving the antiquity of many details in the description which is given in the Priestly Code.

The uniform testimony of our sources with respect to the existence of some kind of sacrificial ritual in earliest Israel can hardly be erroneous, though the constant reaction of the prophets against the formalism and externality of sacrificial cult hardly suggests that undue emphasis was laid upon it in the Mosaic system. The sacrifice of domesticated animals, such as cattle, sheep, goats, and doves, goes back to hoary antiquity and was common to all Western-Asiatic religions from the third millennium B.C. on down; it might thus have passed into Israelite religion in the Mosaic period or later, with numerous other elements borrowed from the sedentary peoples of Palestine. However the part played by animal sacrifice in Semitic religion was so vital that it may be doubted whether Moses could have omitted it from his system without seriously weakening its appeal to worshippers. Among the Semites of antiquity sacrifice was a means of bringing gifts to the deity and of paying him homage which was valid both for a single worshipper and for a group; it served to solemnize every important occasion in the life of a group; and as shown by Bertholet it brought the deity into dynamistic relationship to his worshippers, who became united in flesh and spirit with him by jointly partaking of the sacrificial flesh. Both the substitutional sacrifice, where an animal replaced a more primitive human sacrifice, and the ceremony of the scape-goat (found also in related form in Mesopotamia) emphasized a vital religious concept, that of vicarious atonement for moral transgressions which would otherwise have to be physically expiated by the people.

The problem of the origin of the ethical, civil, and ceremonial laws attributed in later Israel to Moses has been profoundly affected by the appearance of A. Alt's monograph, *Die Ursprünge des israelitischen Rechts* (1934). In this epochal study the gifted Leipzig scholar has distinguished sharply between two main types of pentateuchal legislation: apodictic law and casuistic law. The later is found primarily in the Book of the Covenant (Ex. 21–23), which is a fragmentary legal code of the same class as the Code of Hammurabi (cir. 1750 B.C.), the Hittite Laws (cir. 14th century B.C.) and the Assyrian laws (12th century B.C.). All these codes go back in their basic formulation (provided that . . . then) to the Sumerian jurisprudence of the third millennium. . . . The Book of the Covenant represents the form which the more-or-less common corpus of older customary laws and court decisions took under the special conditions existing in

Canaan, and it probably passed into Israelite hands during the period of the Judges. In the form which it takes in the Book of the Covenant it can hardly be dated before the ninth century. However, it is unlikely that the ninth-century form differed appreciably from its Canaanite prototype many centuries earlier, in view of numerous archaisms in practice and terminology which have older Mesopotamian parallels. The formulation and spirit of the apodictic laws are unique and original in Israel; those of the casuistic laws are at home throughout Western Asia. Besides the Ten Commandments, which best illustrate the spirit of the apodictic laws, we have many other examples, such as the old list of curses imbedded in Deut. 27 and miscellaneous warnings that certain sins must be punished by death, in different parts of the Pentateuch. The most striking thing about the apodictic laws is their categorical character, which stands in sharp contrast to their nearest extra-Israelite parallels, the Egyptian Negative Confession and the Babylonian *Shurpu;* the Israelites are commanded *not* to commit sin, *because Yahweh so wills.*

Of course, we cannot say how many of the apodictic laws actually emanate directly from Moses, but the fact that they cannot be paralleled in this form outside of Israel and that they were believed by different schools of traditional thought in Israel to go back to the time of Moses is sufficient indication that they are in accord with the movement which bears his name. Again we must stress the fact that oral transmission of tradition is inherently more consistent and logical in its results than written transmission, since it sifts and refines, modifying whatever does not fit into the spirit of the main body of tradition. . . . In general it subjects detail to mass scrutiny instead of to the examination of a few who may be mentally superior but who are bound to deviate more frequently from accepted standards. The apodictic law of Israel was not so refined nor so all-inclusive as the Negative Confession of the Egyptians about 1500 B.C., nor did it lay so much

stress on social solidarity as the Babylonian *Shurpu* of somewhat later date; on the other hand, it reflects a much more advanced standard of conduct in many respects. Vicious religious customs, such as child sacrifice, necromancy, and sodomy (which formed part of certain religious ceremonies in the ancient Near East), are forbidden; work on the sabbath, which endangered the physical and mental health of workers (as we know from the recent experience of occidental nations), was prohibited; the worship of all gods save Yahweh and the careless use of His name were banned. As Alt has pointed out, there is nothing in this legislation that conflicts with conditions in Israel under Moses. In this respect it is very different from the Book of the Covenant, which presupposes organized sedentary society. As he has shown, an independent and very important testimony to the antiquity of the apodictic code is provided by the fact that it was annually recited in connection with the Feast of Tabernacles at Shechem.

Having sketched the certain or probable content of the Mosaic system, let us consider possible sources of its teaching. That it was a true "teaching" (*doctrina,* in the empirical, not in the philosophical sense, of course) may be considered as virtually certain, in view of its traditional name *tôrah,* its traditional content, and the fact that the slightly earlier system of Akhenaten was also known as the "teaching" (*sbâyet*). Since Moses bore an Egyptian name and according to tradition had reached a place of considerable social importance in Egypt in his early life, his original *tôrah* may well have contained Egyptian elements which later disappeared before the impact of native Hebrew conceptions. Some of these elements seem still to persist, though we cannot be absolutely sure of any one case, owing to the absence of direct documentation or of complex borrowings from Egyptian sources. Among such possible Egyptian influences may be mentioned: 1. The concept of the god who is sole creator of everything and the formula from which his name, *Yahweh*, was derived (cf. Amun-Reʻ and his litany in the New Empire); 2. The concept of a single god and the establishment of a doctrine based on monotheism (cf. the Aten); 3. Recognition of the necessarily international, cosmic dominion of the reigning deity (cf. Sutekh-Baal under the early Ramessides). On the negative side it is clear that the religion of Israel revolted against virtually every external aspect of Egyptian religion, including the complex and grotesque iconography, the dominion of daily life in the Nineteenth Dynasty by magic, the materialistic absorption in preparing for a selfish existence in the hereafter.

Turning to assess the influence exerted by native Hebrew religion on Moses, we are faced with the difficulty of determining just what the latter accepted and what was introduced into Yahwism after his death from the older Hebrew stock. Leaving the second alternative aside for the moment, since it has been partly stressed above and will be emphasized again in other respects below, we can distinguish a number of clear Hebrew factors — and they are what gave Yahwism much of its vital power over the hearts and minds of Israel: 1. The close association between god and worshipper(s), illustrated by the giving of personal names and by sacrificial rites; 2. The contractual relationship between the deity of a tribe and his people, as illustrated by the constant use of the word *berîth*, "covenant," in early Israel (specific forms of this contractual relationship may be later); 3. The association of terrestrial manifestations of deity with storms and mountains, and the identification of Yahweh with Shaddai, "The One of the Mountain(s)"; the adoption of the stories of the Fathers as part of Israel's inheritance, and the identification of Yahweh with the God of the Fathers; specific appellations of deity and perhaps the nucleus of the cosmogony of Genesis, though the latter may again have been developed later from the native stock of myths and legends.

There is no clear trace of any West-Semitic influence of characteristically Canaanite type on the earliest religion of Israel. After the occupation of Palestine, however, this influence became more and more significant, as we shall see below. How remote early Hebrew tradition was from Canaanite influences may be illustrated by the total absence from it of any story of the conflict between the creator and the dragon at the beginning of world-history. After the seventh century B.C. we find such references becoming more and more frequent and the myth of the victory of Yahweh over Leviathan ultimately obtained wide popularity in rabbinic literature.

In bringing this chapter to a close we have yet one question to answer: Was Moses a true monotheist? If by "monotheist" is meant a thinker with views specifically like those of Philo Judaeus or Rabbi Aqiba, of St. Paul or St. Augustine, of Mohammed or Maimonides, of St. Thomas or Calvin, of Mordecai Kaplan or H. N. Wieman, Moses was not one. If, on the other hand, the term "monotheist" means one who teaches the existence of only one God, the creator of everything, the source of justice, who is equally powerful in Egypt, in the desert, and in Palestine, who has no sexuality and no mythology, who is human in form but cannot be seen by human eye and cannot be represented in any form — then the founder of Yahwism was certainly a monotheist.

Moses as Monolatrist

THEOPHILE JAMES MEEK

Born in 1881, Theophile James Meek was Professor of Oriental Languages
at the University of Toronto from 1923 until 1952. He was one of the five
translators responsible for the University of Chicago's distinguished *The Old
Testament: An American Translation*.

Aᴍᴏɴɢ ᴄʀɪᴛɪᴄᴀʟ scholars today there
is none who claims monotheism for
anyone earlier than Moses, but there are
some who do claim it for Moses, and of
these W. F. Albright is unquestionably the
most outstanding. His argument is a
lengthy one, but not at all convincing. In
one place he says, "The only time in the
history of the ancient Near East when we
find monotheism in the leading cultural
centers, Egypt and Babylonia, is about the
fourteenth century B.C.; it is also then that
we find the closest approach to monotheism
in Syria and Asia Minor. Since it is now
an historical commonplace that we find
similar ideas emerging simultaneously in
different parts of a given cultural con-
tinuum, we should expect to find Israelite
monotheism somehow emerging about that
time" — viz., in the time of Moses, according to Albright. The argument is most unconvincing, and the statement can be
challenged at a number of points. There
was no great, onrushing movement toward
monotheism in the Near East in the fourteenth century, such as Albright affirms.
There is no evidence that Syria and Asia
Minor were more monotheistic then than
at any other period. The texts from Asia
Minor do not show this, nor do the Ras
Shamra texts, to which Albright apparently
has reference. El may have been a great
High God to the people of Ugarit (ancient
Ras Shamra), but along with him were
hosts of other deities, many of them little
less important than he. We have already
noted that the Babylonians and Assyrians
never became real monotheists, and they
were no more monotheistic in the fourteenth century than they were later. As a
matter of fact they were less so, because the
texts over the following centuries show an
ever-growing tendency to emphasize one
god to the exclusion of the others (monolatry), or through the absorption of the
others (henotheism), so that the most
monotheistic of the texts date considerably
after the fourteenth century. The only real
monotheist in the ancient Near East was
Akhenaten of Egypt (and some scholars
question this), and he had no great following. What following he got was obtained
by force; his movement was as much political as religious, and he made so little impression upon his own people that his
religion was stamped out as a vicious heresy
immediately following his death after a
brief reign of only seventeen years. Instead of helping the cause of monotheism
Akhenaten killed it by bringing the Egyptian movement toward monotheism to a
head too soon, by making too great a break
with the old religion, by resorting to force
to establish his religion, and by dying too
soon, leaving no efficient successor to carry
on his work. If Akhenaten was not able

to convert his own people in his lifetime, it is surely unthinkable that he was able after his death to impress an alien like Moses, particularly when Moses lived, as Albright agrees, in the period of bitter reaction against Akhenaten.

However, even though Moses and his people were surrounded on every side by the most monotheistic of peoples, it would not follow at all that they would become monotheistic themselves, nor is there a necessary presumption to that effect. In contrast with the tiny flicker of monotheism which momentarily developed in Egypt in the time of Akhenaten is the dominating role of the resurrection idea throughout her whole history, and yet this idea, which had everything in favor of its adoption, made no impression whatsoever on the Hebrews or any others of the ancient Near East. It is one of the enigmas of history that the Hebrews were so little affected by the religion of Egypt, when both history and archaeology show such intimate contacts between the two. Albright protests that "the history of religion in Israel was not a microcosmic reflection of the evolution of religion in world-history; it was just as homogeneous and as much an organic entity as the history of religion in Egypt, in Babylonia, or in ancient Rome," and yet he would derive Israel's monotheism from a hypothetical world movement instead of having it grow out of its own roots in Israel, in and out of its own environment, influenced no doubt by world thought, but largely independent of it — a monotheism that became the religion not of a single man or a few religionists, but of a whole people, and a monotheism that was strictly monotheistic, as the others, with the possible exception of Akhenaten's, were not. Albright protests against giving a unitarian definition to the word "monotheism," but the only acceptable use of the word is in its dictionary sense, and it is Albright and his kind, rather than his opponents, as he affirms, who are "highly misleading" when they read into a word a meaning that it cannot and should not bear.

We heartily endorse Albright's dictum that "the history of Yahwism in Israel, north and south, becomes unintelligible unless we accept the clear evidence of Israelite tradition"; but Israelite tradition nowhere says or indicates that Moses was a monotheist — not even in Albright's sense of the word. Since we have no autobiography of Moses, it is impossible to say with certainty what he did or did not believe. At best the Old Testament account can only be credited with general and not with detailed accuracy, and in that account the most explicit statement on the subject attributed to Moses is the first command in the Decalogue. There is no certainty of course that this command originated with Moses or that it was known in his day, but we can probably grant Albright's contention that it is in general accord with the movement that bears his name. However, the most that we can claim for Moses in it is monolatry. Neither here nor anywhere else does he deny the existence of gods other than Yahweh, nor does he assert the sole existence of Yahweh, and not having done that, he cannot be called a monotheist. Even Professor E. O. James, who is an anthropologist as well as an Old Testament scholar, with decided leanings toward the theory of primitive monotheism, has to acknowledge that the command asserts nothing more than monolatry and not pure monotheism, and so conservative a churchman as the late Bishop Gore has to concede that it neither proves nor disproves either monolatry or monotheism. The Lutheran Church is one of our most conservative denominations and yet one of its theological professors, Harold L. Creager, writes concerning the First Command in its official organ, *The Lutheran Church Quarterly*: "In neither case [of two possible translations, "in addition to" and "in preference to"], of course, is there any teaching here of monotheism, but only of henotheism. The possibility of worshipping other gods, either along with Jehovah or as entirely displacing him, is distinctly contemplated." Identical are the views of other leading conservative scholars.

Albright translates the command as follows: "Thou shalt not prefer other gods to me." This rendering, he asserts, agrees with the plain meaning of 'al pānāi in several other passages; e.g., Gen. 16:12; 50:1; II Kings 13:14; Deut. 21:16. But in these passages the only one that can possibly have the meaning for which he argues is the last, and even here another possible rendering of the expression in question is "to the disadvantage of" and this has as good support as "in preference to." The expression is one that appears rather often in the Old Testament, but unfortunately with a great variety of meanings; e.g., "over," "in front of," "in the presence of," "on an equality with," "alongside of," "to the disadvantage of," "in preference to," "in addition to," "in defiance of," "during the lifetime of." In most occurrences the particular meaning intended is indicated with more or less certainty by the context, but in the case of the First Command the context is altogether too slight to indicate explicitly what meaning was intended. The whole command reads literally, "Since I, Yahweh, am your God who brought you out of the land of Egypt, out of a state of slavery, there must not be to you any other gods against my face," and no meaning that anyone has yet suggested for the last phrase indicates anything other than monolatry. Even if we follow Albright's rendering, the words can mean only that there are other gods beside Yahweh, but the Hebrews are to prefer none of these to him because it was he who showed himself to be their particular God by rescuing them from bondage in Egypt. Albright stands quite alone in his contention that there is any evidence here for monotheism.

Another statement attributed to Moses, but questionably so, is Deut. 6:4, which is usually translated, "Hear, O Israel, Yahweh our God, Yahweh is one," whatever that may mean. If it makes any sense at all, it seems to mean that there was only one Yahweh and not many, as there were of the Baals. According to the conservative Jewish scholar, Jacob Hoschander, the words "express the Unity of the Lord as far as Israel was concerned, and do not imply the doctrine of an absolute Monotheism, which denies the very existence of all other gods." Against the popular rendering both grammar and syntax require the translation, "Hear, O Israel; Yahweh is our God, Yahweh alone," but even so there is again nothing to suggest anything more than monolatry. This is fully confirmed by other statements which the Old Testament attributes to Moses; e.g., Deut. 4:19: "Beware, when you lift your eyes to the heavens and see all the host of the heavens, the sun, the moon, and the stars, that you do not let yourself be allured into paying homage to them and serving them, whom Yahweh, your God, has allotted to all the peoples everywhere under the heavens." Albright tries to avoid the plain implications of this passage by affirming that it says only that the heavenly bodies have been assigned by Yahweh to all nations alike, but he has to acknowledge that the usual interpretation is possible. It is surely the *only* possible one. From the early rabbinical commentators down to the present day the plain meaning of the passage has been taken to be that Yahweh allotted the gods to the various nations, and that is confirmed by the unequivocal terms of Deut. 29:25, which Albright completely ignores: "They [the Hebrews] went and served alien gods and paid homage to them, gods of whom they had no experience and whom he [Yahweh] did not allot to them." In these two passages Yahweh is represented as a great High God assigning to the different peoples their deities, but this is far removed from monotheism. Most polytheistic peoples have great High Gods; the Sumerians had two, An and Enlil, and likewise the people of Ugarit, El and Baal.

Nowhere in his writings does Albright mention the tradition that connects the bronze serpent of the wilderness with Moses. It is by no means certain that this tradition has any basis in fact, but it is as well attested as other traditions connected with Moses that Albright accepts. The story (Num. 21:4*b*–9) belongs to the JE document and is further supported by the reference in II Kings 18:4. The striking fact about the story and the other stories connecting Moses with the serpent is that they reflect as dynamistic a conception as any cited by Albright for the most primitive form of religion, and that assuredly does not favor a monotheistic religion for Moses. Neither does the statement in II Kings 18:4 that the bronze serpent made by Moses was worshiped right down to the time of Hezekiah. If Moses was the monotheist that Albright makes him out to be, tradition would assuredly never have connected him with the bronze serpent.

In summarizing his arguments for the appearance of monotheism with Moses, Albright says, "If the term 'monotheist' means one who teaches the existence of only one God, the creator of everything, the source of justice, who is equally powerful in Egypt, in the desert, and in Palestine, who has no sexuality and no mythology, who is human in form but cannot be seen by human eye and cannot be represented in any form — then the founder of Yahwism was certainly a monotheist." Of these several items only one or two have any real bearing on the question of monotheism. All the polytheistic peoples of the ancient Near East had cosmic gods and thought of their chief god as creator of everything, equally powerful for his own people in all lands, human in form, and rarely, if ever, seen by human eye. It is true that in the records as preserved to us Yahweh has no sexuality and little or no mythology. This is likewise true of the early Chinese gods and is accordingly no evidence for monotheism. It is very debatable whether Moses taught that Yahweh could not be represented in any form. He may have done so, but even that would not make him a monotheist. Until the coming of Buddhism into their land the Chinese had no images of their gods, nor did the early Aryans of India, and there is reason to believe that the Assyrians had no image of their chief god Ashur. This leaves only one item, the contention that Moses taught the existence of only one God, and there is no evidence of this. It is purely a subjective inference without historical basis, because we do not have enough verifiable information about Moses to know exactly what he did teach.

Albright argues that the stories of Moses, transmitted orally for four centuries or more before being put into fixed form, are at least as historically reliable as the accounts of Zoroaster and Gautama, which were transmitted much longer by oral tradition, and in this he is perfectly right. As a matter of fact, however, we have little dependable information about either Zoroaster or Gautama. Indeed we have so little about Zoroaster that we cannot even date him with any certainty, and the data for his religion are so obscure and so conflicting that no two specialists agree in their interpretation of the evidence, as Albright himself recognizes. There was a time when we had complete and detailed biographies of every great religious leader: Moses, Jesus, Zoroaster, Gautama, Laotze, Confucius, Muhammad, and the others. Modern historical criticism, however, has reduced these biographies to very small proportions, and that of Moses has shared the fate of all the others. If modern historians cannot agree (as they cannot) about the life and teachings of men so recent in history as Lincoln and Washington, concerning whom we have such abundant contemporary records, and hence cannot speak with certainty about them, it is surely most presumptuous on our part to say that we can speak with certainty about Moses. There is much of truth in what Albright has to say about tradition, but it can never have the accuracy that he accords it, and in this we are not hypercritical, as Albright asserts; we are simply realistic. Even contemporary written records are always biased and hence not absolutely accurate, as modern historians are discovering in the case of Lincoln and Washington and hosts of others. In the last analysis the best approach to an understanding of what Moses actually taught must be the psychological one. We do know something of the milieu in which Moses lived and we are pretty well agreed about that milieu — that toward the end of the second millennium B.C., somewhere in the southern Negeb, he gathered about himself a number of wandering tribes and consolidated them into a religious and political confederacy and thus laid the foundations for the nation and its religion. But monotheism to be monotheism must transcend national limitations; it must be supernational and universal. The difference between Moses and Paul was that Paul was an internationalist. By no possible stretch of the imagination can it be said that the outlook of Moses was international. That would have been utterly impossible for him in the environment in which he found himself. He did the one thing that the situation demanded and the one thing to which his followers were in a position to respond. He organized them into a confederacy or amphictyony, and he made the god Yahweh the God of the amphictyony and in his name he made a covenant with the people that Yahweh was to be their confederate god and they were to be his people. This was monolatry and not monotheism. It was the selection of one god out of many for exclusive worship by a particular group as a group, and such theological particularism, as always, was the inevitable growth and accompaniment of a political particularism. As Principal W. C. Graham has well said, "Modes of theological thought never establish themselves as disembodied ideologies. They develop along with and inside of corresponding institutional structures." This point cannot be too strongly emphasized, and yet Albright has completely ignored it. A world concept politically, a world view is the necessary prerequisite to the idea of a world god. In the time of Moses the Hebrews were just learning to take their first steps in the direction of nationalism and were still a long way off from internationalism. They could not possibly reach up to a world concept or a world god. It may be said with considerable assurance that Moses sowed the seeds

of monotheism, but the real fruitage did not come until centuries later because it could not. An idea cannot be born in a day; it comes only "in the fullness of time."

The new thing that came with Moses was not the worship of Yahweh to the exclusion of all other gods, but the united allegiance of a number of tribes to Yahweh as their confederate god, Yahweh being to the confederacy as a whole what the tribal god was to the tribe. This is monolatry and is quite like the monolatry that we noted in Babylonia, Assyria, Egypt, and elsewhere in the ancient world, and Albright is definitely wrong when he asserts that "no religion even remotely comparable to it appeared, and Mosaism remained absolutely unique." Even by the time of David Yahweh had become nothing other than the national god of the united Hebrew state in exactly the same way as Rē became the national god of Egypt, or Marduk of Babylonia, or Ashur of Assyria, or Chemosh of Moab, or Milcom of Ammon, or a host of other gods that could be mentioned. Neither Moses nor David nor any other early Hebrew conceived of Yahweh as being the god of any other people than the Hebrew people. The early tribes had thought of Yahweh as the great High God, but now he was brought down from heaven to earth to become a state god, and so his people came to conceive of him as confined territorially to the land that they occupied. Hence, when David took refuge with the Philistines to escape the jealous persecution of Saul, he felt that he could not take Yahweh with him into Philistine territory but must there worship the Philistine gods (I Sam. 26:19 f.). With greater imagination Naaman of Syria in the time of Elisha conceived the idea of taking two mule loads of Palestinian dirt with him so that he could take Yahweh with him to his homeland (II Kings 5:17).

Even in the land that the Hebrews occupied Yahweh was by no manner of means the only god recognized and worshiped. He was the state god and for him Solomon built a state temple in Jerusalem, but that did not prevent Solomon from worshiping and building temples to other gods (see, e.g., I Kings 11:3 ff.). Over and over again the later prophets condemn their own and earlier generations for the worship of gods other than Yahweh. Hebrew personal names with god elements other than Yahweh prove beyond all question the worship of many gods, as likewise do the excavations in Palestine. The cult that became particularly popular, especially in the more agricultural north, was the fertility cult, and nothing is found in such abundance by the excavator as the paraphernalia of this cult. It was the most natural thing in the world that the Hebrews, as they settled on the land, should have adopted the gods of the land. In fact it was absolutely necessary that they should do so, if they were going to live on the land at all and enjoy its fruits. The gods of the land would have taken offense if they had been ignored, even as Yahweh did in a later period when the deportees brought into Israel by the Assyrians ignored him (II Kings 17:25 ff.). As gods of the land the local deities controlled its productivity. Yahweh, it was true, was the supreme god by right of conquest, but his department was the larger one of the state and not the affairs of ordinary, everyday agricultural and commercial life. In a word, the early Hebrews, in so far as we are able to discover, were no more monotheistic than any other ancient people in the same stage of development.

And yet there was a force making for monotheism with the Hebrews that was not found elsewhere, and that was the new type of prophet that developed in the time of Samuel, the *nābi'* type as against the earlier seer, the *rō'ēh* and *hōzēh*. The latter type was found all over the ancient world, but the *nābi'* type in many of its aspects seems to have been peculiar to the Hebrews. It was characterized by a spirit of intolerance, such as we find, for example, in Deut. 11:16: "Take care lest you become so tolerant [*lit.*, lest your mind become so open] that you turn aside and serve other gods and pay homage to them."

This was an attitude that was unusual in the ancient world and was found elsewhere only with Akhenaten, and it did not come from him to the Hebrews. It had its own independent origin, growing out of its own peculiar circumstances, the oppression of the Hebrews by the Philistines. Like Muhammad, the early Hebrew prophets, the *nĕbi'im*, made the propagation of their religion and the establishment of the Hebrew state an identical project, and so they went up and down the land preaching [a] politico-religious crusade against the Philistines. . . . So intensely devoted were they to Yahweh and his cult that they resented the intrusion of alien gods and stigmatized their worship as disloyalty to Yahweh and the Hebrew nation. Thus they became intolerant of all other cults, and that note of intolerance thus gained was never completely lost. When it was on the point of disappearing with the professionalization of prophecy, the rebirth of prophecy that came in the person of Elijah and his successors revived it with renewed vigor. Prophecy with the Hebrews was a protest or protestant movement — a protest against alien cults and against the settled life on the land that was so largely responsible for the adoption of those cults. To the prophets and kindred orders, like the Nazirites and Rechabites, the olden time with its simple nomadic life and its simple monolatrous religion was the best time. Agricultural life, commercial ties, and treaty relations with other peoples had brought in other cults to divide the religious loyalty of the people, and that they resented.

This would seem to give support to Albright's contention that the prophets were in no sense innovators, but simply revivers of the old Mosaic religion; that they had nothing whatever to do with initiating monotheism or anything else in Yahwism; they simply revived the old. This surely is a low estimate of the prophets, but it is in line with Albright's view that Mosaism did not change in fundamentals from the time of Moses to the time of Christ. What the prophets did, according to him, was to strip popular Yahwism of its Canaanite accretions and restore it to its pristine purity. He compares the work of the prophets to the Protestant Reformation in Christianity and the Wahhabi movement in Islam. It is true that the Protestant reformers thought that they were restoring the original form of Christianity, even as 'Abd al-Wahhab thought that he was restoring the original religion of Muhammad, but every historian knows that neither the one nor the other did anything of the sort. They simply established what they *thought* was the original religion. It is true, as Albright notes, that most of the nations of the Near East in the time of the later prophets were looking back with nostalgia to their more glorious past and were trying to revive it by imitating such things as the ancient script and language (which was nothing but sympathetic magic), but again we have to note that their efforts to recover the past were without success because of their deficient knowledge of the past. In a way the Book of Deuteronomy represents a similar effort on the part of the Hebrews; it may indeed have been "a conscious effort to recapture both the letter and the spirit of Mosaism which, the Deuteronomists believed, had been neglected or forgotten by the Israelites of the Monarchy," as Albright believes, but even he hardly dares assert that they actually did recapture the letter and spirit of Mosaism, for he goes on to say that Deuteronomy clearly follows the *direction and development* already marked out by J and E, and a little later he speaks of the "cult of Yahweh as reconstructed for the Mosaic age by the Deuteronomic school." The Deuteronomists may have tried to recapture the original Mosaism, but after all it could only have been their idealized picture of the past that they produced. All peoples everywhere and in all times have idealized their past, and so did the Hebrew people. There is no question but what the prophets thought and professed that they were reviving the old religion, but it was only their idealized reconstruction of that religion. This is apparent, among other

things, from their claim that the ancient religion of Moses was without sacrificial rites of any kind (e.g., Amos 5:25; Is. 1:12; Jer. 7:21 ff.; Is. 43:23 f.). But one of the claims that Albright makes for Moses is that much of the sacrificial system must go back to him. If the prophets idealized the Mosaic religion with respect to its ritual, we have every reason to believe that they idealized it in other respects as well, and this is what scholars have long since maintained. More or less unconsciously the prophets read back into the past what they wanted for their own time, bolstering up their own ideas of what ought to be with the sanctity and authority that always belong to the past — a form of argument that is as old as man. Luther may possibly have thought that he was no innovator, but such he was, nevertheless, and so were the Hebrew prophets. Each made his contribution to the continuing stream of Hebrew religion and this stands out clearly as one reads the writings in chronological order. Indeed one cannot read Albright's own account of them, each in turn, without feeling the onward movement of the religion.

To the Hebrew prophets Yahweh was a jealous god who insisted upon having his people all to himself. As Elijah put it, if Yahweh was to be the people's god, they must follow him; if it was to be the Baal, then they should follow him: "How long will you go limping on two opposite contentions; if Yahweh is God, follow him, but if the Baal, follow him" (I Kings 18:21). The choice must be between the two; it could not include both, as was the case with other peoples. Yahweh was not like Marduk or Ashur or Rē or the usual run of ancient god, who was always ready to admit another cult along with his own so long as his own rights were not infringed. Even between Amun and Aten there was no great hostility until Akhenaten proceeded to displace Amun by Aten. With conquests and alliances and the adoption of new occupations the regular practice of the ancient world was to admit the gods of the conquered or allied states or the new occupations into their pantheon, but as subordinate gods to the state god, exactly as the conquered or allied states became subject states to their own; but the Hebrew prophets would brook no such admission. They insisted upon preserving the monolatry of the old nomadic days and would have one state god for the state, as previously the tribe for its simple life had had one tribal god. This was not monotheism, but an extension of earlier tribal monolatry to the state, and it reached its culmination finally in the revolution of Jehu, who not only made Yahweh the state god of Israel, but definitely attempted to suppress all the other cults, as related in II Kings 10. This account may not be true in all its details, but there is no question but that Jehu made a really serious attempt to stamp out the old Baal religion — a religious persecution that was unparalleled in the ancient world. After the eclipse of Yahwism in the time of Jeroboam I it was once again established as the official religion of the north, and the north was now independent of the south. For the first time in history we have here two distinct and independent, in fact two hostile, peoples worshiping one and the same god as state god, and in this a long step had been taken in the direction of making Yahweh an international and so a universal god, and that further step was taken by the eighth-century prophets.

With other religions we noted a tendency to monotheism as the theologians came to interpret the various gods as simply forms or manifestations of the one chief god. It was monotheism by syncretism, if indeed it can be called monotheism at all. Strictly speaking it was not monotheism, because no effort was made to suppress any of the minor or local cults or priesthoods, or any of the local features of the cults. The several cults continued as always, with no change except the identification of the local god with the state god. The movement was pantheistic and henotheistic, but not reformatory. Not so was the propaganda of the Hebrew prophets. Thoroughgoing as Jehu's revolution had been, they were not

satisfied with it, because he continued the cult of the golden calves, reinterpreting them simply as images of Yahweh. Here was syncretism somewhat after the order of the ancient world and the sort of thing that the common people could understand, because they had long since been giving their children names reflecting this syncretism, names like Baaliah . . . , "Baal is Yah," and Egelyo . . . , "The calf is Yaw." But this was not acceptable to the later prophets and they condemned it, because it was to them simply the old bull cult under a new name; and because the images harked back to the old cults, they would have none of them and they came to condemn idolatry in all its forms and all the licentious practices that went with it. Hence, unlike Elisha, Hosea had no word of praise for Jehu, but condemnation only (1:4), and in 13:1 f. he says:

> Whenever Ephraim spoke there used to
>   be awe;
> He was a prince in Israel.
> Then he incurred guilt through the Baal
>   and died;
> And now they keep on sinning,
> In that they have made for themselves
>   molten images
> Out of their silver, by their skill, idols,
> Wholly the work of craftsmen.
> "To such," they say, "sacrifice!"
> Men kissing calves!

And again in 8:5 ff.:

> Hateful is your calf, O Samaria;
> My anger blazes against them [*i.e.*, its
>   makers].
> How long will they be incapable of
>   innocence?
> For it is the creation of Israel,
> Since a craftsman made it,
> And it is not god.
> Verily, Samaria's calf
> Shall become splinters;
> For it was wind they sowed,
> And a whirlwind they shall reap.

Similar polemics are found in Hos. 4:17 f.; 12:12; 13:2; and Amos 4:4, and likewise in II Kings 20:29 ff., the prophetic writer of which approved of much that Jehu did, but condemned him for his preservation of the golden calves. To prevent the contamination of Yahwism by the idolatry and licentious rites of the local cults the prophets were led in time to oppose worship of any kind at the high places, because its inevitable effect upon the people was to produce a syncretism of the local cults with Yahwism, and that the prophets resisted. With might and main from the time of Amos onward they fought the practice, until eventually they obtained its absolute prohibition in the Book of Deuteronomy, and the Yahweh religion was centralized in one national sanctuary by Josiah, shorn of all heathen associations, or so it was supposed (II Kings 23:3–24:27).

Like the earlier prophets, Hosea saw that it was the agricultural life that had weaned the people away from Yahweh to the fertility cult of the bull-god, the Baal, but unlike them he saw the futility of preaching a god that was simply an austere desert god. If Yahweh was to be accepted, he must be presented as a god whom the people needed, a god to meet their requirements, in short a fertility-god. So Hosea took over the idea of marriage with deity, which was such a prominent feature of the popular religion, ethicized it, and gave a new interpretation of the old covenant idea, making it now a marriage rite with Yahweh. Since the agricultural life had led to the corruption of Baalism, he would wrench the people from the soil and return them to their earlier Bedouin life of the desert; then in the desert they would return to Yahweh as in the olden days, and Yahweh would once more betroth them to him and bring them back to their own land. The soil would again be tilled, bountiful harvests would result, and the people would learn at last that it was Yahweh and not the Baals who gave the grain and wine and oil: "And it shall come to pass on that day," it is the oracle of Yahweh, "that you will call me 'My husband,' and you will no longer call me 'My Baal.' For I will put away the names of the Baals from her [Israel's] mouth, and they shall no longer be invoked by their name" (Hos. 2:16 f.). Thus Hosea disengaged the life of agriculture from the perils that threatened the religion and succeeded in making an alliance between civilization and the religion of Israel, and he succeeded also in commending Yahweh to his people, divorced from all licentious practices, idolatry, and magic rites. It was syncretism of a sort, more properly eclecticism. Hosea took the meat, but left the shell. He took what was vital in the popular cults, appropriated it for Yahweh, and surcharged it with spiritual meaning.

The establishment of Yahweh as the god of two distinct nations like Judah and Israel, and the recognition that he could use an alien people like the Assyrians as an instrument of punishment against his own people when they failed him, eventually led the prophets to see in Yahweh a god of the world, a god universal. So far as we can discover Amos was the first to regard Yahweh as the god of peoples other than the Hebrews, but he nowhere denies the existence of other gods nor does he say anywhere that Yahweh alone is god in the world. Neither does Hosea, nor Micah, nor First Isaiah, nor Zephaniah. More and more, however, the prophets were underrating the alien gods, and this despite the fact that as Assyria grew strong public opinion rated its gods higher and higher, until Ahaz was moved to introduce their worship on a small scale (II Kings 16:10 ff.), and Manasseh on a large scale (II Kings 21:1 ff.). To save Yahweh from the oblivion of his people the prophets had to liberate Yahweh from his people and make him the god of the world, who for his own beneficent purpose exalts, now this people, now that people, to the end that all may know him and obey him. To Isaiah, accordingly, the rival gods were but 'ĕlīlīm, worthless creatures, vain and unavailing (Is. 2:8, 18, 20; 10:10 f.; 19:1, 3; 31:7). This was theoretical monotheism, which very quickly blossomed into the practical, thoroughgoing monotheism of Jeremiah and Second Isaiah, who declared in most emphatic terms that Yahweh alone was God and all the so-called gods had no real existence at all; they were merely figments of the imagination, the creation of man himself (see, e.g., Jer. 5:7; 10:2 ff.; 16:20; Is. 41:21 ff.; 44:9 ff.). This was monotheism of a kind that none among the neighboring nations ever attained, with the possible exception of Akhenaten of Egypt. But Hebrew monotheism was surely not derived from him. Similarity or even identity of ideas does not necessarily imply borrowing. Faced with similar problems under similar conditions, it is only natural that men should make similar responses, no matter what the age or what the nationality. Hebrew monotheism grew up in its own way with the Hebrew prophets, in and out of its own environment, influenced no doubt by world thought, but largely independent of it. It was the crystallization of an earlier Hebrew movement, even as that of Akhenaten was of an earlier Egyptian movement, and there is nothing to indicate that the one grew out of the other.

It was not until the time of Jeremiah and Second Isaiah that a thoroughgoing monotheism was possible with the Hebrews. Imperialism was in the air, and "monotheism is but imperialism in religion." There had been a succession of world empires — first the Assyrian, then the Babylonian, and now the Persian. Was there likewise a succession of World Gods? Or was there one World God directing the course of world history? It was left to Second Isaiah to answer this and he did so in no uncertain terms, particularly in chapters 41 to 48. Over and over again he ridicules the idea that there can be more gods than one and for the first time in history we have a man preaching the religious solidarity of mankind, as much interested in the well-being of other peoples as in his own. And yet the one god of the world is the Hebrew God Yahweh, but in Second Isaiah Yahweh loses in large part his earlier character as the national god of Israel and becomes instead the Universal God, and in his effort to express that more adequately Second Isaiah often uses a term for deity that has no national connotation whatsoever, . . . literally "He," "the One who is."

The Hebrew prophets began as champions of Yahweh. That led them to oppose all alien cults, and bit by bit that led them to the position that Yahweh alone was God. With them monolatry blossomed into monotheism, nationalism into universalism, and religion became a matter of the heart and of righteous living rather than mere ritualistic practice. With them developed a new interpretation of god, a new interpretation of man, and a new interpretation of religion. With them origins ceased and the fruitage of ages of intensest religious experience was given to mankind of those mighty oracles which still remain the wonder and admiration of the world.

A Rejoinder

WILLIAM FOXWELL ALBRIGHT

A GENERATION after Ezekiel came the great unknown prophet whose collected poems were attached to the anthology of Isaiah — possibly because he bore the same name (which was common in that age, as shown by a number of other biblical and inscriptional occurrences). The exact extent of the writings of Deutero-Isaiah is uncertain; competent opinion ranges from Torrey's view that chapters 40–66 are substantially a unit to Duhm's complicated dissection. The general opinion of scholars is that Isa. 40–55 forms a unit, coming from the period just before and just after Cyrus's victory over Nabonidus of Babylon (539 B.C.). In two respects Deutero-Isaiah marks the culmination of the Mosaic movement as such: in his clear-cut and sweeping definition of the concept of ethical monotheism and in his doctrine of vicarious suffering.

It is frequently asserted that true ethical monotheism does not appear in the Old Testament before Deutero-Isaiah. This statement is very misleading, as the reader may conveniently see for himself by examining the exhaustive classification of pertinent data made by Count Baudissin as long ago as 1876. Unmistakable claims of world-power and uniqueness for Yahweh appear with the earliest known rhapsodist prophets, Amos and Hosea, and become frequent in Isaiah and Jeremiah. Along with them appears outspoken repudiation of pagan deities and their claims. For instance, Amos and Jeremiah call pagan deities "lies" and "falsehood"; Isaiah and Jeremiah call them "vanities" and "illusions"; Jeremiah and the Deuteronomic school call them "no-gods"; Ezekiel, the Deuteronomists, and Jeremiah call them *gillûlîm*, which seems to mean properly "pellets of dung." This list is surely opposed to the idea that pagan deities were conceded real existence by the prophets. If we had poems or sermons from the climax of the prophetic movement in the ninth century B.C., we should doubtless find the same attitude toward the claims of pagans for their deities. The words of Elijah in I Kings 18:27 or in II Kings 1:6 have a flavor of ironic pragmatism which is quite characteristic of early Israel . . . ; it was enough for the prophet to deny the pagan god any power, after which the question of his existence became an unimportant consideration. As a matter of fact there is no single utterance in pre-exilic sources which sounds as polytheistic as the assertion of the Chronicler (II Chron. 2:5, which is not taken from Kings but is quite original with the Chronicler) that "our God is greater than all the gods." Yet few would claim that orthodox Jewry was polytheistic in the fourth century B.C.! In the second century B.C. the Jewish author of Aristeas declares that the God of Israel is identical with the Greek Zeus and about the same time the translators of the Septuagint render various Hebrew terms for pagan gods as "demons" (*daimônia*). Moreover, the Book of Enoch says that the pagan cults were introduced by fallen angels and this conception was generally held both by rabbinical theologians and by the early Church Fathers. Philo Judaeus sees no harm in identifying the Hellenic gods and demons with Jewish angels and in regarding all of them as emanations of the divine essence, forming a bridge between God and man.

From William Foxwell Albright, *From the Stone Age to Christianity*, 2nd ed. (Baltimore: 1946), pp. 250–252. Reprinted by permission of The Johns Hopkins University Press.

In order to understand the view-point of Yahwistic thinkers of the Prophetic Age (since we cannot directly control the ideas of their predecessors), we must bear in mind that they lived in an age of empirical logic, many generations before the dawn of systematic philosophical reasoning. Nowhere in the prophetic writings of pre-exilic times is there any hint of cosmic speculation. The prophets were not interested, so far as we can tell, in how the world had come into existence or how the forces of nature operated; it was quite enough for them to know that God controlled them. They had a real moral interest in knowing why God did certain things, but the idea that any of God's actions were subject to general physical laws which man might discover by observation and reasoning was totally foreign to them, as it was to all pre-philosophical thought. Similarly it was enough for them to know that pagan deities had no real power and could be over-ruled at any time by Yahweh: whether their existence was real or only nominal, whether they were angels or demons or simple illusions mattered little, since they were in any event evil or powerless. By the middle of the sixth century B.C. all was changed for the orthodox Jews; they were now living in the Diaspora, among idolaters, where it was increasingly difficult for worshippers of Yahweh to preserve their faith and that of their families. No compromise was longer possible; either the pagan gods existed or they did not exist, and if they did not exist it was well to sweep away all other intermediaries between the invisible spiritual lord of the universe and His people Israel. The pure ethical monotheism of Deutero-Isaiah would have been too rarefied a faith to have had permanent religious value if it were not for His doctrine of the infinite kindness and generosity of God, who feeds his flock like a shepherd, who carries the lamb in His bosom and gently leads pregnant ewes (Isa. 40:11).

Moses as the Source of Monotheism

H. H. ROWLEY

Born in 1890, Harold H. Rowley was educated at Bristol Baptist College, Bristol University, England, and was Professor of Hebrew Language at the University of Manchester from 1945 to 1959. His books include *From Joseph to Joshua* and *The Faith of Israel*.

ONE OF THE current issues in Old Testament study is concerned with the antiquity of Israelite monotheism. The view has long been common that monotheism began with the eighth century prophets and became explicit with Deutero-Isaiah. Causse attributed the beginnings of monotheism to Elijah, but Hölscher rejects this view on the ground that in the religion of Elijah none of the theoretical consequences of monotheism are found. There is no denial of the existence of other gods

From H. H. Rowley, *From Moses to Qumran, Studies in the Old Testament* (New York: 1963), pp. 35–63. Reprinted by permission of Association Press (New York) and Lutterworth Press, Ltd. (London).

and no universalism. Pfeiffer goes so far as to deny any real monotheism before Deutero-Isaiah. He says: "We can only speak of monotheism in the Old Testament before Second Isaiah by using the word in some other sense than the belief that there is only one god." More often, however, the beginnings of monotheism have been found in the teachings of the eighth century prophets, and I. G. Matthews says that it was the conception of the brotherhood of man which we find in the teaching of Amos which was the foundation of ethical monotheism. This view is commonly associated with the name of Wellhausen, whose evolutionary presuppositions in the field of the history of religion are widely discarded today, and who is held responsible for the idea that polytheism gradually evolved into monotheism through the influence of the prophets. Actually this idea is older than Wellhausen, but it was doubtless under his influence that it became widespread. Writing in the *Zeitschrift für die alttestamentliche Wissenschaft* in 1925 W. L. Wardle said: "It may still be regarded as the prevailing view that Israel's religion passed gradually from an elementary stage of animism, totemism, fetichism, through the stage of tribal deity, to the stage represented by the religion of the prophets, and that this stage was reached only under their influence." Wardle added that there were signs of revolt from this view. Long before this, however, there were scholars who were more cautious, and who, while recognizing development in Israelite religion, did not ascribe it to natural evolution, but to the seed of monotheism which was implanted in Israel's religion by Moses, and which grew to its full flower under the influence of those men of God whom we know as the prophets.

Today there are many challenges to the evolutionary view, which is held in some quarters to be sufficiently discredited by being connected with the name of Wellhausen. That all of Wellhausen's views can no longer be maintained is true. It is equally true that no living teacher can be sure that all of his views will be maintained unchanged for almost a century. That Wellhausen was wrong in some of his presuppositions may be agreed; but that all his views were false is a presupposition as illegitimate as any with which he started. Hence, while I disagree at many points with Wellhausen and his school, I do so with respect and remember my debt to the men with whom I disagree. To build the tombs of the prophets of old and to stone contemporary prophets is a practice which stands condemned in the Gospels; to throw stones at the tombs of the scholars of a former generation is no more worthy an occupation.

One of the views which has come into fashion in recent years maintains that monotheism goes back to the beginnings of the human race. This view is not new, of course. It was advanced as a scientific hypothesis by Andrew Lang. It was presented by that distinguished Biblical scholar, M.-J. Lagrange, who held that the original Semitic religion was a monotheism in which El was worshipped, but that El was later split up into a multiplicity of gods. More particularly, however, this view is associated with the name of Wilhelm Schmidt, the author of the voluminous work *Der Ursprung der Gottesidee*. Schmidt seeks to establish the thesis that the more primitive a people is, the more nearly it approaches monotheism, which must therefore have been the original faith of man. Polytheism is held to be the fruit of the disintegration of monotheism, and to be associated with the advance of culture. Presuppositions as unwarranted as those of the evolutionary school appear to lie behind this view, which rests on a pessimistic view of human culture. I once heard Wheeler Robinson scornfully describe it as the view that monotheism is the religion of people who cannot count beyond three. To suppose that peoples whom we call "primitive" preserve the earliest outlook of mankind is an assumption that is without foundation. Schmidt observes that these peoples have never played any important part in the world, and his work would seem to be directed to the establishment of the remarkable thesis that primitive monotheism was the religion of the insignificant, and that its retention entailed permanent insignificance. Moreover, such monotheism as can be ascribed to "primitive" man by these means is an arid faith in a God whose characteristic is his "onliness." Vague qualities are attributed to him, but at the best he is a shadowy Providence. Religion is to be tested by the character, and not merely by the number, of the gods, and Biblical monotheism is more than the belief that God is one and beside Him is no other. Such "primitive monotheism" as this theory sets out to prove is quite other than Biblical monotheism.

In an important study the Swedish scholar H. Ringgren has shown that two opposite tendencies are found in religion, the one moving from polytheism to monotheism and the other moving from monotheism to polytheism. By the hypostatization of qualities and functions a single god can disintegrate into many, while by various processes many may give place to one, the character of the consequent monotheism varying according to the process whereby it is achieved. It may advance from polytheism through a monarchic theism to monotheism, or it may take a pantheistic form, or become the abstraction τὸ θεῖον. While, then, the dogmatism that assumes a linear development of religion towards monotheism is wrong, it is equally impossible to assume a development away from primitive monotheism. The question is not to be determined either way on grounds of general principles, but on grounds of evidence, and it is doubtful whether adequate data exist to recover with security the original religion of man.

Our concern here, however, is not with primitive monotheism but with Biblical monotheism, which is certainly not derived from the supposed primitive monotheism. A much more important challenge to the view with which we started is the claim that Moses established monotheism in Israel. This challenge is important because it claims no less a scholar than W. F. Albright amongst its champions. In his brilliant work *From the Stone Age to Christianity* he presented this view, after some preliminary indications of it, and several other scholars have followed him. Yet actually, as Meek has shown, Albright only established Mosaic monotheism by giving a new connotation to the term monotheism. He says: "If the term 'monotheist' means one who teaches the existence of only one God, the creator of everything, the source of justice, who is equally powerful in Egypt, in the desert, and in Palestine, who has no sexuality and no mythology, who is human in form but cannot be seen by human eye and cannot be represented in any form — then the founder of Yahwism was certainly a monotheist." Most of the elements of this definition are irrelevant to the question of monotheism, and of the one vital element there is no evidence. For nowhere in the Pentateuch is Moses credited with the formal denial that any other gods exist, such as we find in Deutero-Isaiah, save in passages such as Dt. 4:35, 39; 32:39, which quite certainly did not issue from Moses.

On the other hand, no evidence can be provided to show that polytheism developed into monotheism in Israel by natural evolution or by philosophic speculation. There is no evidence that Moses was a polytheist in the sense that he practised the worship of many gods; yet there is no evidence that he was a monotheist in the sense that he denied the existence of more than one God. Yahweh was to be the only God for Israel, and Him only were they to serve. This would seem to lead to the conclusion that he was a henotheist, and it is undeniable that henotheism was found in Israel in the post-Mosaic period. Albright dismisses Jg. 11:24, which he calls the "parade example," on the ground that it stands in a speech addressed to an alien people and arguing with them on the ground of their ideas. It is less easy to dismiss 1 Sam. 26:19 f., where David, in speaking to Saul, says that the driving of him away is the same as telling him to go and worship other gods. Nor need we be surprised that henotheism was found in Israel. For we find ample evidence that many in Israel declined from the height of the religion of Moses and fell into polytheism.

It is scarcely sufficient, however, to say that Moses was a henotheist, and in any case this would still leave us with the problem of the transition from henotheism to monotheism. Moab and Ammon are commonly said to have been henotheistic, the one holding Chemosh to be Moab's god and the other Milkom to be Ammon's. Actually we have no evidence that Chemosh alone was worshipped in Moab and Milkom alone in Ammon, and it may well have been that while these were worshipped as the national gods, others stood beside them, just as in Israel through long periods Yahweh was regarded as the national God, though other gods were popularly worshipped alongside Him. Even if Moab and Ammon were henotheistic, however, we should still have to ask how it was that Israel became monotheistic and they did not. No profound and enduring influence on the religion of mankind came through them, whereas it did through Israel.

It is on this account that it is necessary to go beneath labels in our study of Israelite monotheism, and to perceive that if Moses was less than a monotheist he was more than a henotheist. I have already said that some older writers maintained that in the work of Moses lay the seed of monotheism. Similarly Meek says: "It may be said with considerable assurance that Moses sowed the seeds of monotheism." It is this that I would emphasize more than many writers have done, and this that offers some justification for the over-emphasis of Albright. Moses did much more than lift Israel to the religious level that is so often ascribed to Moab and Ammon. On the human side he is the creator of Israel's religion, giving it a character all its own. For Israelite monotheism developed less out of the "onliness" of Yahweh as the legitimate object of worship than out of His character. The outstanding work of Moses in this connection is not so much the teaching that Yahweh was to be the only God for Israel as the proclamation that Yahweh was unique.

There is ample evidence that before the time of Moses Israel was polytheistic. Her whole environment was polytheistic. Egypt and Babylon were both polytheistic, and we now know much of the pantheon of the people of Ugarit, who have provided us with our fullest insight into the ancient causing so much trouble in Palestine in Canaanite religion. The Ḥabiru, who were the fourteenth century B.C., and who are identified by some with the Hebrews entering the land under Joshua, were polytheistic. For we find references to "the gods of the Ḥabiru." Many of the personal names which we find in Israel testify to the polytheistic background out of which they emerged. Alt has argued that each of the patriarchs, Abraham, Isaac, and Jacob, had his own special God. Moreover, while in the Old Testament Shaddai, El, Elyon, and Yahweh are all equated and identified, it is hardly to be denied that they were once regarded as separate deities.

The Egyptian heretic king, Akhenaten, is often supposed to have been the source of Mosaic monotheism. Even Albright has lent some countenance to this, saying: "A priori, we shall expect that Israelite monotheism would come into existence in an age when monotheistic tendencies were evident in other parts of the ancient world, and not at a time when no such movements can be traced. Now it is precisely between 1500 and 1200 B.C., i.e. in the Mosaic age, that we find the closest approach to monotheism in the Gentile world before the Persian period." The evolutionary presuppositions of this statement will not escape notice. It is commonly said that Akhenaten was a monotheist, because he suppressed the worship of all gods save one in Egypt. It is not certain, however, that he was a genuine monotheist in the sense of believing that only one God existed, and that therefore He was the only legitimate object of worship for all men. Mercer, indeed, denies that he was a monotheist. In all true monotheism universalism is involved, and there is little evidence that Akhenaten was concerned with the world that lay beyond his empire. His religious reform is believed by some to have had a political, rather than a genuinely spiritual, basis. Yet even though we allow that Akhenaten was a monotheist, it does not follow that Moses was influenced by his ideas. For if Moses took an important step on the road to monotheism, he took it along an entirely different road from that of Akhenaten, whose religion fell far short of the significant heights reached by Moses.

The religious achievement of Moses was not something that grew naturally out of his environment or circumstances, and the ideas that he mediated to Israel were not derived from Egypt or from any other people. Certainly they were not ideas that were floating around in that age. "The real source of Hebrew monotheism," says Wardle, "we should probably find in the religious experience of Moses which underlies the tradition of Exodus 3." Here we read that Yahweh sent Moses into Egypt to a people that did not worship God by the name Yahweh, to announce that He had chosen Israel and would redeem them from their bondage. Later, when the people came out of Egypt, they repaired to the sacred mount, where the covenant bond was established between Israel and God. This covenant was the pledge of loyalty given by Israel in response to the deliverance already achieved. This was quite other than the bond between Chemosh and Moab, and it is this which distinguishes Mosaic religion from ordinary henotheism.

It is commonly believed that Yahweh was the God of the Kenites before He became the God of Israel. In recent years it has been claimed that the divine name Yahweh is found at Ras Shamra, where Yw figures as the son of El. This is very uncertain, however, and for our purpose is of little importance, since it is unlikely that the Israelites took over their worship of Yahweh from the people of Ugarit. That the name Yahweh is older than the time of Moses, however, there is little reason to doubt. It is easy to find a contradiction between Exod. 6:2 f., which states that God was not known to the patriarchs by the name Yahweh, and passages in Genesis, which represent God as saying to the patriarchs "I am Yahweh." It is less easy to estimate the significance of this contradiction. Obviously both cannot be precisely true. It has long been held, however, that the Israelite incursion into Canaan was in two waves, widely separated in time. Only one of these waves could have been led by Moses, and it could well be that he introduced the worship of God under the name Yahweh to the group he led, while the group he did not lead reached its worship of Yahweh otherwise. There could thus be substance in both of the traditions preserved in the Bible, and it is only the attempt to impose a unity on them and to make them tell of a single stream of history that is responsible for the contradiction.

It is improbable that the Israelites had worshipped Yahweh from time immemorial. Had they done so, and had the tribes that came out of Egypt been connected with the tribes that were not in Egypt by both blood and faith, there would have been no room for any tradition that Moses mediated Yahwism to them. So far as the tribes that were led by Moses are concerned, it is scarcely to be doubted that he introduced them to the worship of Yahweh as their God. It is true that by syncretism he identified Yahweh with the God their fathers had worshipped, but in so doing he made it clear that Yahweh was a new name by which they were to worship their God. This does not mean that it was a completely new name for God, first heard on the lips of Moses. The name may not have been an unknown name even to the Israelites in Egypt, though it was not the name they had hitherto used for their own God.

I have already said that it has long been a common view that Yahweh was the God of the Kenites before He was the God of

Israel. Jethro, the father-in-law of Moses, was the priest of a God whose name is not given. So far back as 1862 it was suggested that he was the priest of Yahweh. While this view has been rejected by a number of scholars, and cannot claim to be certain, it seems to me to have all probability on its side. And in the absence of conclusive evidence we can only be guided by probabilities. We are not told the name of Jethro's God; but we are told that when Moses came out of Egypt with the Israelites, Jethro came to meet him, and that he was highly elated at the demonstration of the power of Yahweh in the deliverance of Israel. "Now I know that Yahweh is greater than all gods," he cried. Buber objects that he could hardly have said this if Yahweh were his own God, for no one would make such an implied confession about his own God. But this is scarcely cogent. Whatever belief in the power of Yahweh he might have cherished in the past, this unique demonstration of His power was something that could only have lifted it to a higher degree of knowledge and certainty. Buber supposes that Jethro was so impressed by this demonstration of the power of Yahweh that he forthwith identified his own God with Yahweh, but of this there is no hint in the story. Meek, on the other hand, thinks that Jethro was converted to the worship of Yahweh by this proof of His power. Yet again, not only is there no hint of this in the story, but the sequel gives quite another impression. For Jethro offers sacrifice, and presides at the sacred meal which follows. Buber here stresses the fact that the sacrifice is offered to Elohim and not to Yahweh, but it can hardly be supposed that the demonstration of the power of Yahweh in the deliverance of the Israelites would lead forthwith to the sacrifice to some other god. Nor is it clear why Jethro should officiate as priest and preside at the sacred feast unless his own God was being approached. If, however, it were his own God, it would be clear why he should preside. For none but he was a properly initiated priest of his God.

In the sacred feast we should then have the first incorporation of the Israelite leaders into the worship of Yahweh. Certainly there is nothing in the story to suggest that Jethro was being initiated into the worship of Yahweh, as Meek supposes; for it is unusual for a novice to preside at his own initiation.

Further, Jethro gives to Moses instruction and advice as to the administration of justice, which was regarded as a religious rather than a civil function. All of this suggests that Jethro was acting not merely as the father-in-law of Moses, but as the priest. For Moses is not represented as a youth, needing riper experience to guide him in managing the people. The man who had stood before Pharaoh and who had led Israel out of Egypt was not lacking in personality or natural wisdom. On that side there was little that he needed from Jethro. But of technical knowledge pertaining to the priestly duties Jethro could speak.

A Dutch writer, C. H. W. Brekelmans, has offered some criticism of what I have published on this subject, and has suggested that Jethro was a chief rather than a priest, and that he came to meet Moses to supplicate for a treaty with him. The sacrifice is said to have been for the ratification of the treaty. Of this there is once more no suggestion whatever in the story. Brekelmans says it may have been the custom for the suppliant for the treaty to preside at the meal which marked its ratification. But it can hardly be supposed that it was customary for the suppliant for a treaty to give instructions as to how justice should be administered. Brekelmans says that if Jethro had offered priestly instructions they should have been offered to Aaron and his sons rather than to Moses. But this is to ignore the fact that up to this point there had been no suggestion that Aaron was to be appointed to the priestly office. Jethro would have needed prophetic foresight, as well as priestly knowledge, for this.

That the Kenites were Yahweh worshippers is suggested by other passages. Cain is the eponymous ancestor of the Kenites, and he is said to have borne the mark of Yahweh upon him. Moreover, in the days of Jehu's revolution, Jonadab, the son of Rechab, is a devotee of Yahweh, and we learn from the book of Chronicles — itself confessedly late — that the Rechabites were of Kenite stock. The same passage associates the Calebites and the Kenites. To this we shall return below.

It has been claimed that there is one item of extra-Biblical evidence supporting the Kenite hypothesis. This is in the form of an Egyptian text in which the place name Yhw is found, referring to a spot quite certainly in the neighbourhood of Kenite settlements, and dating from the time of Rameses II. Amongst the other places mentioned in the context are Seir, Laban, and Sham'ath, all of which have Edomite or Midianite connections. It is of particular interest to note that this text is dated *circa* 1300 B.C., in the age to which I assign the life and work of Moses, and Grdseloff, who published the text, observed that it renders the Kenite origin of Yahwism more probable.

I cannot here discuss how this illuminates the whole complex of Israelite tradition. The tribes which pressed into the land from the south in the pre-Mosaic age included Judah and some Kenite and Calebite elements, as we are told in the Bible. If these were Yahweh-worshipping people, the worship of Yahweh might have spread from them throughout the group of associated tribes by infiltration. There was no moment of dramatic acceptance of the worship of Yahweh, any more than there was any moment of the dramatic acceptance of Baal after the settlement of Israel in Canaan. Hence, in the southern corpus of traditions which we know as J, the worship of Yahweh is represented as going back to the beginnings of time. These tribes were not with Moses, and in their traditions the beginnings of Yahwism in Israel are not connected with him. On the other hand, the tribes that came out of Egypt with Moses were introduced to the worship of Yahweh by him and by the Kenite Jethro, after a memorable experience of deliverance, followed by the covenant of Sinai. The tribes led by Moses consisted principally of the Joseph tribes, and it is not therefore surprising that in the northern corpus of traditions, which we know as E, the beginnings of Yahwism are associated with Moses. The divergence between the two traditions is not, therefore, a meaningless contradiction. There is substance behind both.

It is sometimes suggested that the name of Moses' mother is the Achilles' heel of the whole Kenite theory. For she was called Jochebed, and this name appears to be compounded with the divine name Yahweh. If, then, Moses' mother bore a theophorous name compounded with Yahweh before he was born, it cannot be supposed that he introduced the name Yahweh to the Israelites who were in Egypt. To counter this argument it is sometimes noted that our evidence for the name Jochebed is found only in the late Priestly source, or even that it is not certain that it is compounded with Yahweh. It is unnecessary to resort to either shift. If there were Yahweh-worshipping Kenites associated with the Israelites who entered Canaan from the south in the pre-Mosaic age, it would not be surprising for there to be some intermarriage between the associated tribes. Amongst these tribes there were some Levites, and such intermarriage could bring a Levite family into association with a Kenite family, and so bring a Kenite name into a Levite home. It is probable that the Levites and the Simeonites in this early wave of immigration reached Shechem, where they were guilty of some act of treachery, now reflected in Gen. 34, as the result of which they were "scattered in Israel," as the Blessing of Jacob indicates. Some of the Levites then appear to have gone into Egypt, and amongst them the ancestor of Moses' mother, who had married a Kenite woman. It is well known that names tend to recur in families, and this Kenite name might have been passed down to become the name of Moses' mother, without involving any worship of Yahweh. This means that there was probably some Kenite blood in Moses, though derived at a distance through his mother.

This in turn explains why Moses fled to Jethro when he was forced to flee from Egypt. When Jacob left home through fear of his brother's wrath, he fled to his mother's kindred. For Moses to do the same would therefore be most natural. If he knew that his mother was of Kenite descent, he could repair to a Kenite settlement without fear, knowing that he had some claim on them.

It is often supposed that the Kenite theory of the source of the divine name Yahweh reduces the work of Moses to the mere mediation to the tribes he led of the religion of his father-in-law. Nothing can be farther from the truth. If Yahwism was the worship of the Kenites from time immemorial and none knew how it had begun amongst them, then it was fundamentally different for the tribes Moses led by the mere fact of the unforgettable experience through which they were led to it. It was always associated amongst them with the memory of the deliverance they had experienced. Moreover, it is not to be supposed that Moses simply transferred to Israel the Yahwism of his father-in-law without change, and that such development as took place in their religion in the course of time just happened by itself with the mere passing of the years. It is antecedently likely that under the influence of a great leader, and in the circumstances of Israel's adoption of Yahwism, some new quality would be given to their faith.

Yahweh had first chosen Israel in her weakness and oppressed condition, and had sent Moses in His name to rescue her from her bondage, though she did not hitherto worship Him. Then Israel in her gratitude pledged herself to this God in undeviating loyalty. That her pledge was not always kept is clear from the record of the Old Testament itself, but the taking of the pledge was a new and highly significant thing in the history of religion. Meek here objects that there was nothing new in this,

since many a people has adopted another religion. It is perfectly true that there have been many cases of the adoption of a foreign religion. Sometimes it has been imposed upon a subject people, or even readily adopted because of the prestige of a powerful people; sometimes, as in the case of Kenite religion among the southern tribes, it has spread by gradual penetration among peoples closely associated with one another, and intermarrying with one another; sometimes by infiltration from a neighbouring people, as frequently in the story of Israel. But here there is nothing of such a character. Here Israel's adoption of Yahweh was the response to His adoption of Israel, and the sequel to His achieved deliverance of her. Israel's covenant with Yahweh in the time of Moses was based on what God had done, and on Israel's gratitude for His deliverance.

It is probable that Moses gave a new Decalogue to the tribes he led. It is well known that in Exod. 34 we have what was once most probably a more primitive Decalogue than that contained in Exod. 20 and Dt. 5. In its present form we have more than ten commands in Exod. 34, but probably there were originally ten. This decalogue, the Ritual Decalogue as it is often called, is usually assigned to the J document, which is associated with those southern tribes that Moses did not lead. Morgenstern thinks this decalogue was a Kenite decalogue. I have argued that it was of Kenite origin, though it has come to us through Israelites whom Moses did not lead, and who may have gradually modified some of the original provisions after their entry into Canaan, and who may have added the agricultural festivals, which would not figure in the old Kenite Decalogue. On the other hand, Moses gave to the tribes he led another Decalogue, which is now expanded into the two forms it has in Exod. 20 and Dt. 5. This is often called the Ethical Decalogue, because it is more interested in conduct than in ritual, and even penetrates to the spring of conduct in motive. It does not seem unreasonable to me that a new Decalogue with a higher quality should be given to Israel by Moses when a Covenant based on gratitude, which is itself an ethical emotion, as fear and anger are not, was being mediated. Hence I do not take the view that the work of Moses is to be resolved into the mere mediation to Israel of the religion of the Kenites. The divine name Yahweh was probably taken over, and the forms of the religion; but a new spirit was given to the religion and a new level to its demands. The sense of Yahweh's election of Israel, of His deliverance, of His claims upon her obedience, were all new, and through the truly prophetic personality of Moses it was established on a higher basis than Kenite religion had reached. That difference of level may be realized by the comparison of the two Decalogues.

In all this there are the seeds of monotheism. The God, or gods, hitherto worshipped by the Israelites were identified with Yahweh, and ceased to count as against Him. There was no conflict between Yahweh and them. He just gathered them into Himself, and in so far as they had characteristics different from His, they ceased to have meaning for Moses. The name of Israel's God was henceforth Yahweh; but His character was not derived from her own or from Kenite traditions so much as from the redeeming acts which had brought blessing to Israel.

Here it is important to distinguish the syncretism of this process from ordinary syncretism, and particularly from the syncretism that identified Yahweh with Baal. There was always an undercurrent of feeling that Yahweh was not Baal, and in any time of national revival this found expression. Yahweh never gathered Baal into Himself, and refused to be swallowed up by Baal. Yet we never find any conflict between Yahweh and the God, or gods, of the patriarchs. They were negligible, save in so far as they were identified with Yahweh. All other gods, worshipped by other peoples, were entirely negligible. The gods of Egypt figure in the story of the deliverance of Israel, but Yahweh's conflict is not with them, but with Pharaoh; and they could be dropped from the story without varying its course. This is not monotheism, and there is no reason to attribute universalism to Moses. Yet here we have surely the seeds of both. It is not that Yahweh is merely supreme amongst the gods, their monarch and lord, to whom they are all subordinate. It is that all other gods are negligible beside Him or against Him.

Moreover, Yahweh's power was not limited to a single land. He could be active in Egypt or in Palestine as freely as in His chosen seat. A God who could thus be active wherever He wished, who could claim for Himself whatever people He wished, and beside whom no other gods counted, was no tribal or national god, and certainly not merely one of a host of gods. His "onliness" might not be affirmed; but His uniqueness is manifest. If He is not the only God, He is certainly more than one example — even the most important example — of the category of gods. Among all the gods He alone mattered, and He could do with Israel or with any other people what He would.

This is not monotheism, and it is unwise to exaggerate it into monotheism. Nevertheless, it was incipient monotheism and incipient universalism, so that when full monotheism was achieved in Israel it came not by natural evolution out of something fundamentally different, but by the development of its own particular character. In substance, therefore, this view is much closer to the view of Albright than to the evolutionary view with which I began, though it refrains from ascribing full monotheism to Moses. The development that followed was a development of the seed which Moses had already planted, and which came into Mosaic religion through the experience of Moses and the people, and not from any *Zeitgeist* or upsurge of the human spirit. Moreover, when development came, it came through the personalities of the prophets, who can hardly be regarded as the expression of the Israelite life of their day. With the eighth and seventh century prophets we find incipient monotheism giving place increasingly to a more specific belief, and in Deutero-Isaiah we find the explicit formulation of monotheism with undeniable clarity. The antiq-uity of monotheism in Israel may therefore be dated from the time of Moses, provided it is recognized that it was but the germ of monotheism in his day, when a new impulse of incalculable significance to the world came into religion.

The Nature of Yahweh

MARTIN BUBER

Martin Buber was born in Vienna in 1878. From 1924 to 1933 he was a professor of comparative religion at the University of Frankfort, but in 1933, when Hitler came to power, Buber left Germany. After temporary residence in several countries, he settled in Jerusalem, where he was a member of the faculty of the Hebrew University from 1938 until 1951. A prolific writer on biblical themes, Buber joined Franz Rosenzweig in producing a German translation of the Old Testament, entitled *Die Schrift*. Buber died in 1955.

IT IS A FUNDAMENTAL ERROR to register the faith with which I deal as simple "Monotheism." Here may be applied what was written half a century ago by Paul Yorck von Wartenberg to the philosopher Wilhelm Dilthey, his friend and my master: "I should consider it desirable for an attempt to be made to disregard all these categories, Pantheism, Monotheism, Theism, Panentheism. In themselves they have no religious value whatsoever, being only formal and of quantitative character. They reflect views of the world and not views of God, and constitute only the outline of an intellectual attitude; and only a formal projection even for this." It is not so decisive whether the existence of a Unity exalted over all is assumed in one's consideration, but the way in which this Unity is viewed and experienced, and whether one stands to it in an exclusive relationship which shapes all other relations and thereby the whole order of life. Within the so-called Monotheism the concrete difference of the images of God and the vital relations with God made incisions which are sometimes far more important than the boundaries between a particular "Monotheism" and a particular "Polytheism." The universal sun-god of the imperialist "Monotheism" of Amenhotep IV is incomparably more close to the national sun-god of the ancient Egyptian Pantheon than to the God of early Israel, which some have endeavoured to derive from him.

What is important for us about this God of Moses is the association of qualities and activities which is peculiar to Him. He is the One who brings His own out, He is their leader and advance guard; prince of

From pp. 9–10, 13, 39, 41–55 of *Moses: The Revelation and the Covenant* by Martin Buber (New York: 1958). Reprinted with the permission of Rafael Buber and of Harper Torchbooks, Harper & Row, Publishers, Inc., New York.

the people, legislator and the sender of a great message. He acts at the level of history on the peoples and between the peoples. What He aims at and cares for is a people. He makes His demand that the people shall be entirely "His" people, a "holy" people; that means, a people whose entire life is hallowed by justice and loyalty, a people for God and for the world. And He is and does all this as a manifesting, addressing and revealing God. He is invisible and "lets Himself be seen," whatever may be the natural phenomena or historical process in which He may desire to let Himself be seen on any given occasion. He makes His word known to the men He summons, in such a fashion that it bursts forth in them and they become His "mouth." He lets His spirit possess the one whom He has chosen, and in this and through this lets him mature the work divine. That Moses experiences Him in this fashion and serves Him accordingly is what has set that man apart as a living and effective force at all times.

* * *

In order to learn at first hand who Moses was and the kind of life that was his, it is obviously necessary to study the Biblical narrative. There are no other sources worthy of serious consideration; comparison of reports, normally the chief means of ascertaining historical truth, is not possible here. Whatever has been preserved of Israel's traditions since ancient times is to be found in this one book. Not so much as the vestige of a chronicle dating from that period, or deriving from the nations with whom the Children of Israel established contact on their journey from Egypt to Canaan, has been preserved; and not the vaguest indication of the event in question is to be found in ancient Egyptian literature.

* * *

The section which deals with the Revelation at the Burning Bush (Ex. iii, 1-iv, 17) cannot be regarded as a compilation from varying sources and documents. All that is needed is to remove a few additions, and there appears before us a homogeneous picture; any apparent contradiction can be accounted for by the fact that the text has not been fully understood. The style and composition of this section show that it is the fruit of a highly cultivated dialectic and narrative art; but certain of the essential elements of which it is composed bear the stamp of early tradition. . . .

YHVH sees Moses approach to look; and "God" . . . calls to Moses from out of the bush. . . . It is only now that God tells him who he is; he who communicates with him, Moses, here in strange parts, is none other than the god of his forefathers, the God of the Fathers; and hence, as we may suppose, the God of whom Moses must have heard yonder in Egypt when he went forth every day "unto his brethren."

The favoured "Kenite" hypothesis explains that YHVH was unknown to Israel until then, being a mountain, a fire or maybe a volcanic god and simultaneously the tribal god of the Kenites (who are often assumed to have been wandering smiths) and that Moses had "discovered" this god at his seat of worship on Sinai. This hypothesis is unfounded. There are not the faintest indications that any god of the name was ever honoured in that district. No more than suppositions are possible with regard to the character and qualities of a, or the, putative Kenite god. For this reason the hypothesis has not unjustly been described as "an explanation of ignotum ab ignoto" [the unknown from the unknown]. We know of YHVH's connection with Sinai only from the Bible; and what we know is that at the time of the Exodus of the Children of Israel from Egypt YHVH had selected Sinai as the seat for his manifestation. The Song of Deborah, which is referred to (Jud. v, 5), does not bring YHVH, as is supposed, from Sinai to the Galilean battlefield, it only ascribes the name "a Sinai" to Mount Tabor, from which (Jud. iv, 6) the God who had come in storm clouds out of the south revealed himself in the glorious victory over his foes.

And Elijah, who is thought to have made a pilgrimage to Sinai when he wished to "speak personally to and seek an audience of YHVH," really wandered defeated and weary of life to the mountain in order to lay himself down and perish in "the cave," (1 Kin. xix, 9) that is, in yonder cleft in the rock (Ex. xxxiii, 22), familiar to the wanderers, from which Moses had once seen the God passing by. YHVH never appears in the tales of his revelations to Moses and Israel as "fixed" on Sinai; he only comes down thither on occasion, descending from heaven to do so (Ex. iii, 8; xix, 18, 20). Comparative religion, too, is familiar with mountains not merely as the divine seat, but also as the place where gods manifest themselves.

And just as this does not make him a mountain god, so the fact that in the course of the revelation he often makes use of the element of fire, the heavenly origin of which is frequently referred to in the Bible, does not convert him into a fire god. For our purpose, however, the most important fact is not the traits of the nature gods which he has absorbed (criticism of these particular characteristics is offered in the story of the Sinai revelation to Elijah [cf. 1 Kin. xix, 11 f.]) but what he is to begin with. Is he an alien god whom Moses meets, and through Moses, Israel, and who is made the national god of Israel by Moses? Or is he a "God of the fathers" [Abraham, Isaac, and Jacob]?

The Bible permits us to ascertain this. All we have to do is to compare the peculiarities of the God of Moses with those of the God of the Fathers. More precisely, it is our concern to reveal the peculiar divine likeness, first in the constituents of our tale which, beyond all question, lead back to early tradition, and then in the corresponding elements of the other, a likeness, that is to say, which it is impossible simply to classify by some type or other of the pre-Mosaic religious history of the Ancient East, for despite all its relationships with one or another of these types, it shows a character differing from them all. There-after we must compare the two divine likenesses with one another.

If the material in the Bible is subjected to such an examination, the two likenesses will be found to differ in a special manner; namely, just as a clan god in non-historical situations might be expected to differ from a national god in an historical situation. Yet at the same time it can be observed that both depict the identical god. To begin with the former, the clan god [of Abraham, Isaac, and Jacob]: we immediately observe two main characteristics which are both demonstrated in his relation to the men chosen by him. One is that he approaches these men, addresses them, manifests himself to them, demands and charges them and accepts them in his covenant; and the second, closely connected with the first, that he does not remain satisfied with withdrawing them from their surrounding world and sending them on new paths, but wanders with them himself and guides them along those new paths; meanwhile, however, remaining invisible insofar as he does not "make himself seen" by them. Taken both together, these cannot be compared with the attributes of any other divinity in the history of religion, despite certain analogies of detail. The prerequisite assumption for both is that this god is not bound to any place, and that the seats of his manifestations do not restrict him; above them open the gates of heaven (Gen. xxviii, 17), through which he descends and returns to his inaccessible realm.

We find all this once more in the second likeness, in the national god [of Moses]; but here it has the vivid colour of a historical driving force. The new and supplementary characteristics, striking as they may appear, nevertheless seem peripheral to us when compared with the central power of the common element. Once again the God makes his great demands of his men, commanding and promising, establishing a covenant with them. But now he no longer turns to single persons but to a people, and that people too he leads forth and himself conducts along the new way.

Once again the invisible one becomes manifest from time to time. Once again heaven and earth are joined, and the God utters his words from heaven unto earth (Ex. xx, 22).

This is no alien god "discovered" by Moses on Sinai; it is the God of the Fathers. And yet it is in his eyes none other than the God of whom his wife's kinsfolk may have told him, saying that he dwells on this mountain. When Moses came to the Midianites, he entered the range of life of the Fathers; and he senses the apparition he now sees as being that of the God of the Fathers. As YHVH had once gone down with Jacob to Egypt (Gen. xlvi, 4), so has he now gone from Egypt to Midian; possibly with Moses himself, who was obviously under his protection like Jacob of old. At all events Moses perceives who it is that appears to him; he recognizes him. That was what had happened in the days of the Fathers too. Abraham had recognized YHVH in the El 'Elyon of Melchizedek, YHVH had permitted himself to be seen (Gen. xvi, 7, 13) by Abraham's concubine, the Egyptian maid, Hagar, as the spirit of a desert spring — seemingly one of those divinatory springs at which something can be "seen" during sleep. What happens here, as it had happened there, is, from the point of view of religious history, an identification. The God brought with and accompanying a man is identified with the one known as previously to be found at this spot; he becomes recognized in him. From Babylonian and Egyptian religious thought we know the tendency to give full expression to the faith in the supremacy of a single god by interpreting the other gods as his forms of manifestation. But with the exception of the short-lived imperialistic theology of Amenhotep IV, no serious attempt in this direction was or could be made in the great Pantheons. Only in the religious atmosphere of a solitary exclusive God outside the Pantheons, claiming and leading his own men, could any such identification become a living reality. . . .

After the God tells his chosen one who he is, he reveals the cause and purpose of the message with which he wishes to entrust him. The sentence with which this partial address begins, and that with which it ends, balance one another like the members of a building, through the two keywords *ammi,* my people, and *Mitsraim,* Egypt. These are repeated in both, and denote the subject and the aim of the act: "I have indeed seen the sufferings of my people who are in Egypt," and "lead out my people the children of Israel from Egypt." To attribute the two sentences, as is so often done, to different sources, constitutes a misunderstanding of the entire form and sense of the speech. With this repeated "my people" at the commencement and close of the passage, YHVH recognizes Israel in a fashion more powerful and unequivocal than would have been possible by any other verbal means. To be sure, he has not yet designated himself their God. He will become the God of Israel as a people solely through the revelation to the people; now he wishes to be known only as the God of their forefathers, to whom he had once promised the land whither he would lead Israel. But since he so stresses the naming of Israel as his people, he shows that the bond uniting them had been established of old. No new, no alien god talks in such a way. This likewise indicates the hopelessness of the attempt sometimes made to attribute this first speech, which refers to the patriarchs, to some later stratum of the text. Try to insert at this point the phrase assumed to have been in the original, namely "I am the god," *i.e.* "I am the god of this mountain," and the message, flaming with historical revelation and historical faith, shrinks, one might well say, to a private remark which conveys nothing.

And now begins the great duologue in which the God commands and the man resists. . . .

The resistance offered to the mission, which was opposed to all the natural tendencies of the one charged, and the breaking down of this resistance by the Divine Power, belong, as shown us by the autobiographical notes of Jeremiah and the paradigmatic little book on Jonah (the nucleus of which may derive from the eighth century B.C.E.) to the most intimate experience of the prophetic man.

The first objection, that of his own smallness compared with the vast task, corresponds precisely, after eliminating the supplements, to the third (Ex. iv, 10), in which Moses stresses his difficulty of speech. And once again, after YHVH responds that He, the God of Creation, makes the mouth of man to speak or be dumb, and therefore made Moses himself as he is, and sends him just as he is, YHVH continues: "Go, I myself shall be present with your mouth and shall instruct you what you should say.". . .

It is necessary to bear in mind the two promises of the speaking God which begin with the word *ehyeh*, "I shall be," I shall be present, assuring that he would remain present amid his chosen, in order properly to understand the central part of the duologue, the central question and the central response, framed by these two pillars.

The point at issue here is not Man but God, the name of God. The words of Moses are generally taken to mean that he wished to learn the answer which he would have to give the people if they asked him to tell them the name of the God whose message he brought. Understood in this sense, the passage becomes one of the chief supports of the Kenite hypothesis, since it is scarcely possible to imagine that any people would not know the name of the God of their fathers. If you wish to ask a person's name in Biblical Hebrew, however, you never say, as is done here, "What (*mah*) is his name?" or, "What is your name?", but "Who (*mi*) are you?", "Who is he?", "Who (*mi*) is your name?", "Tell me your name." Where the word "what" is associated with the word "name," the question asked is what finds expression in or lies concealed behind that name. . . .

Moses expects the people to ask the meaning and character of a name of which they have been aware since the days of their fathers. Which name? From the answer of the God it can be seen that the question refers to YHVH.

In a later manifestation (Ex. vi, 3), YHVH informs Moses that he was seen by the forefathers "in El Shaddai," that is, in the quality of a Shaddai God; but "By my name YHVH I did not make myself known to them." What Shaddai is can only be guessed from the word and the circumstances under which it is used in the stories of the patriarchs; yet the name clearly means the Divinity as Power; and, as seems to be indicated by five of the six passages in Genesis where the name is found, as the power making the human clan fruitful. Therefore the term can be taken to imply the power founding the tribe. Here, indeed, the issue is the biological development of Israel, which is understood as a divine work. The name YHVH, it is true, is introduced only once in the Genesis narrative in the form of a direct revelatory speech placed in the mouth of the God (Gen. xv, 7), and in the identical form of phrase with which the revelation to the people begins (Ex. xx, 2). But Abraham proclaims the name when he comes to Canaan as might a herald, at one spot after another (which should not be understood as a calling in prayer), and his clan knows the Name. Is it likely that the author of Exodus vi, 3, did not know this? Here, however, what is said is not that the patriarchs made no use of the name of YHVH, but only that they did not know him in the quality characterized by this name; and that this had now been discovered. What can that mean?

Of all the various suppositions regarding the prehistoric use of the name YHVH there is only one the development of which makes all this understandable without contradiction. To the best of my knowledge it was first expressed nearly half a century ago by Duhm in an (unpublished) lecture at Goettingen: "Possibly the name is in some degree only an extension of the word *hu*, meaning he, as God is also called by other Arab tribes at times of religious revival — the One, the Unnamable." The

Dervish cry Ya-hu is interpreted to mean "O He!", and in one of the most important poems of the Persian mystic, Jelaluddin Rumi, the following occurs: "One I seek, One I know, One I see, One I call. He is the first, He is the last, He is the outward, He is the inward. I know no other except Yahu (O He) and Ya-man-hu (O-He-who-is)." The original form of the cry may have been *Ya-huva,* if we regard the Arabic pronoun *huwa,* he, as the original Semitic form of the pronoun "he" which, in Hebrew as well as in another Arabic form, has become *hu.* "The name *Ya-huva* would then mean O-He! with which the manifestations of the god would be greeted in the cult when the god became perceptible in some fashion. Such a *Ya-huva* could afterwards produce both *Yahu* and *Yahveh* (possibly originally *Yahvah*)." Similar divine names deriving from "primitive sounds" are also known in other religions, but in, say, the Dionysos cult the cries developed into corresponding nouns, whereas the Semites preserved the elemental cry itself as a name. Such a name, which has an entirely oral character and really requires completion by some such gesture as, for example, the throwing out of an arm, is, to be sure (as long, at least, as the undertone of the third person still affects the consciousness of speaker and listener) more suitable for evocation than for invocation. As an invocation it appears in the story of the patriarchs only in a cry (Gen. xlix, 18) which strangely interrupts the continuity of the blessings of Jacob. This may also explain why during the pre-Mosaic period scarcely any personal names are recorded as having been formed with this divine name. The only known exception, as it would appear, is the name of Moses' mother, Yochebed, which apparently means "YHVH is weighty." If so, it might possibly be regarded as a sign of some specific family tradition, which prepares the way for a new relation to the Divine name.

Certainly it is more typical that in the course of the ages, particularly at an epoch of increasing religious laxity, as the Egyptian period appears to have been for Israel, the element of excitation and discharge connected with the calling of the name did not merely ebb away, but the name itself degenerated into a sound simultaneously empty and half forgotten. Under such conditions an hour might well come when the people would ask this question of a man bringing them a message from the God of their fathers: "How about his name?" That means: "What is this God really like? We cannot find out from his name!" For as far as primitive human beings are concerned, the name of a person indicates his character.

But there is also something else included in the question, namely the expression of a negative experience which the enslaved people had had with this God of theirs: "After all, he never troubled about us all this while! When the Egyptians require their gods, they invoke them by uttering their 'true' names in the correct fashion, and the gods come and do what is necessary. But we have not been able to invoke him, we cannot invoke him. How can we be certain of him, how can we bring him into our power? How can we make use of his name? What about his name?"

The "true" name of a person, like that of any other object, is far more than a mere denotative designation for men who think in categories of magic; it is the essence of the person, distilled from his real being, so that he is present in it once again. What is more, he is present in it in such a form that anybody who knows the true name and knows how to pronounce it in the correct way can gain control of him. The person himself is unapproachable, he offers resistance; but through the name he becomes approachable, the speaker has power over him. The true name may be entirely different from the generally familiar one which covers it; it may also, however, differ from the latter only in the "correct" pronunciation, which would also include the correct rhythm and the correct attitude of the body while engaged in the act of pronouncing it; all things which can only be taught and transmitted personally. And

since the true name phoneticises the character of the object, the essential thing in the
last resort is that the speaker shall recognize
this essential being in the name, and direct
his full attention upon it. Where that
happens, where the magical work requires
an aiming of the soul at the being meant,
that is, when the "person" aimed at is a
god or a demon, the fuel is provided into
which the lightning of a religious experience can fall. Then the magical compulsion becomes the intimacy of prayer, the
bundle of utilisable forces bearing a personal name becomes a Thou, and a de-
magisation of existence takes place.

As reply to his question about the name
Moses is told: *Ehyeh asher ehyeh*. This is
usually understood to mean "I am that I
am" in the sense that YHVH describes himself as the Being One or even the Everlasting One, the one unalterably persisting in
his being. But that would be abstraction of
a kind which does not usually come about
in periods of increasing religious vitality;
while in addition the verb in the Biblical
language does not carry this particular
shade of meaning of pure existence. It
means: happening, coming into being, being there, being present, being thus and
thus; but not being in an abstract sense.
"I am that I am" could only be understood
as an avoiding of the question, as a "statement which withholds any information."
Should we, however, really assume that in
the view of the narrator the God who came
to inform his people of their liberation
wishes, at that hour of all hours, merely to
secure his distance, and not to grant and
warrant proximity as well? This concept is
certainly discouraged by that twofold
ehyeh, "I shall be present" (Ex. iii, 12; iv,
12), which precedes and follows the statement with unmistakable intention, and in
which God promises to be present with
those chosen by him, to remain present
with them, to assist them. This promise is
given unconditional validity in the first part
of the statement: "I shall be present," not
merely, as previously and subsequently,
"with you, with your mouth," but absolutely, "I shall be present." Placed as the
phrase is between two utterances of so concrete a kind that clearly means: I am and
remain present. Behind it stands the implied reply to those influenced by the
magical practices of Egypt, those infected
by technical magic: it is superfluous for you
to wish to invoke me; in accordance with
my character I again and again stand by
those whom I befriend; and I would have
you know indeed that I befriend you.

This is followed in the second part by:
"That I shall be present," or "As which I
shall be present" [*asher ehyeh*]. In this way
the sentence is reminiscent of the later
statement of the God to Moses (Ex. xxxiii,
19): "I shall be merciful to him to whom
I shall be merciful." But in it the future
character is more strongly stressed. YHVH
indeed states that he will always be present,
but at any given moment as the one as
whom he then, in that given moment, will
be present. He who promises his steady
presence, his steady assistance, refuses to
restrict himself to definite forms of manifestation; how could the people even venture to conjure and limit him! If the first
part of the statement states: "I do not need
to be conjured for I am always with you,"
the second adds: "but it is impossible to
conjure me."

It is necessary to remember Egypt as the
background of such a revelation: Egypt
where the magician went so far as to
threaten the gods that if they would not do
his will he would not merely betray their
names to the demons, but would also tear
the hair from their heads as lotus blossoms
are pulled out of the pond. Here religion
was in practice little more than regulated
magic. In the revelation at the Burning
Bush religion is demagicized.

At the same time, however, the meaning
and character of the Divine Name itself
changes; that is, from the viewpoint of the
narrator as well as from that of the tradition given shape by him, it is unfolded in
its true sense. By means of the introduction
of an inconsiderable change in vocalization,
a change to which the consciousness of

sound would not be too sensitive, a wildly ecstatic outcry, half interjection half pronoun, is replaced by a grammatically precise verbal form which, in the third person (*havah* is the same as *hayah* — to be — but belongs to an older stratum of language) means the same as is communicated by the *ehyeh*: YHVH is "He who will be present" or "He who is here," he who is present here; not merely some time and some where but in every now and in every here. Now the name expresses his character and assures the faithful of the richly protective presence of their Lord.

And it is the God Himself who unfolds his name after this fashion. The exclamation was its hidden form; the verb is its revelation. And in order to make it clear beyond all possibility of misapprehension that the direct word *ehyeh* explains the indirect name, Moses is first instructed, by an exceptionally daring linguistic device, to tell the people "*Ehyeh*, I shall be present, or I am present, sends me to you," and immediately afterwards: "YHVH the God of your fathers sends me to you." That *Ehyeh* is not a name; the God can never be named so; only on this one occasion, in this sole moment of transmitting his work, is Moses allowed and ordered to take the God's self-comprehension in his mouth as a name. But when, shortly before the destruction of the Northern Kingdom of Israel, the prophet Hosea, in order to give concrete expression to the impending crisis in national history, calls his newborn son *Lo-ammi*, not my people, he justifies this name (Hos. i, 9) with the Divine word: "you are not my people and I am not *ehyeh* for you." One expects to hear: ". . . and I am not your God," but what is said is: "For you I am no longer *ehyeh*, that is 'I am present.'" The unfaithful people lose the presence of their God, the name revealed is concealed from them once again. Just as the *Lo-ammi* refers to the *ammi* of the Burning Bush episode, so does this *ehyeh* refer to that.

Again and again, when God says in the narrative: "Then will the Egyptians recog-

nize that I am YHVH," or "you will recognize that I am YHVH," it is clearly not the name as a sound, but the meaning revealed in it, which is meant. The Egyptians shall come to know that I (unlike their gods) am the really present One in the midst of the human world, the standing and acting One; you will know that I am He who is present with you, going with you and directing your cause. And until the very close of the Babylonian Exile, and later, saying such as "I am YHVH, that is my name" (Is. xlii, 8), or even more clearly, "Therefore let my people know my name, therefore on that day, that I am he who says 'Here I am'" (Is. lii, 6), cannot be otherwise understood. . . .

The meaning of the name is usually ascribed to the "Elohist," to whose source this section of the narrative is attributed. But quite apart from the fact that there was no Elohist in this sense, . . . such discoveries or conversions are not born at the writing desk. A speech like this *ehyeh asher ehyeh* does not belong to literature but to the sphere attained by the founders of religion. If it is theology, it is that archaic theology which, in the form of a historical narrative, stands at the threshold of every genuine historical religion. No matter who related that speech or when, he derived it from a tradition which, in the last resort, cannot go back to anybody other than the founder. What the latter revealed of his religious experience to his disciples we cannot know; that he informed them of what had happened to him we must assume; in any case, the origin of such a tradition cannot be sought anywhere else.

At his relatively late period Moses did not establish the religious relationship between the Bnei Israel and YHVH. He was not the first to utter that "primal sound" in enthusiastic astonishment. That may have been done by somebody long before who, driven by an irresistible force along a new road, now felt himself to be preceded along that road by "him," the invisible one who permitted himself to be seen. But it was Moses who, on this religious relationship, established a covenant between the God and "his people." Nothing of such a kind can be imagined except on the assumption that a relation which had come down from ancient times has been melted in the fire of some new personal experience. The foundation takes place before the assembled host; the experience is undergone in solitude.

The Theme in Its Setting

WILLIAM H. McNEILL

William H. McNeill was born in Canada in 1917. Educated at the University of Chicago and Cornell, he joined the history faculty at Chicago in 1947 and has since become head of the Department of History. His publications cover a wide range of subjects. *The Rise of the West*, from which the following selection is taken, is his most ambitious work.

BIBLICAL TRADITION asserts that Abraham, the ancestor of the Hebrew people, migrated about 1950 B.C. from the Sumerian metropolis of Ur northward to Harran, and thence to Palestine. This story may have a sound basis; and it is possible that the God of Abraham originated as a family deity, one of the small gods of ancient Sumer.

The distinctive beginning of Hebrew religion, however, must be dated from the time of the exodus from Egypt. Only a part, perhaps a small part, of the Hebrew people had sojourned in Egypt, departing for the desert sometime in the thirteenth century B.C. under the leadership of Moses. Their abrupt change in mode of life from forced labor on public works to wandering in the wilderness — reversion though it undoubtedly was to an ancestral nomadic pattern — required explicit lawgiving. The years in Egypt must have eroded ancient customs; and Moses' followers were probably of varied origins, lacking any single traditional leadership and organization.

It was natural, indeed inevitable, that Moses' lawgiving should take religious form, and there is no reason to doubt the essential accuracy of the biblical account of how, after making good the escape from Egypt, Moses ascended Mount Sinai to commune with Yahweh and returned with a simple code of law — the Ten Commandments. The people's formal acceptance of the Commandments constituted their covenant with Yahweh, whom they recognized henceforth as their divine guardian and supreme authority.

When the tribe that Moses had thus reformed took its place in Palestine side by side with other Hebrew tribes, the religion of Yahweh and the Mosaic law offered a valuable rallying point for the larger community. The other tribes, having recently come from the desert, presumably lacked written law, regular priestly organization,

Reprinted from *The Rise of the West* by William H. McNeill, pp. 158–166, by permission of The University of Chicago Press. © 1963 by The University of Chicago.

or definite revealed religion. Under the conditions of the conquest and early settlement of Palestine, they soon began to feel the need for such supplements to traditional tribal organization and custom, and, finding a suitable system ready at hand among a kindred and neighboring people, readily adopted the religion of Yahweh and made it their own.

The turn to agriculture involved a basic shift in mode of life, with profound political and religious repercussions. Politically, the need for defense against both nomadic neighbors to the east and the formidable Philistines to the west led in the eleventh century to the rise of the Hebrew monarchy. Religiously, the worship of Yahweh increasingly gave way to fertility cults, which had been indigenous to Canaan before the arrival of the Hebrew tribesmen. After all, Yahweh was a god of the desert and of war, and when life came to depend on agriculture, it seemed logical to resort to those divinities — the Baals — which had of old proved their efficacy by promoting the fertility of the fields.

Yahweh's role as the national war god kept his worship alive, for there was frequent need to call upon his aid in battles against neighboring peoples. The military enterprise by which Saul established the monarchy therefore had the incidental effect of exalting the cult of Yahweh; and even though David, Solomon, and their successors in the divided kingdoms of Israel and Judah proved hospitable to foreign worships, the religion of Yahweh remained vigorously alive. In particular, Yahweh by common consent took precedence over all others gods in time of public emergency.

Civilization in all its aspects penetrated among the Hebrew people in the days of the monarchy. To be sure, the Mosaic prohibition of graven images inhibited the development of art; but the Hebrews' literary achievements more than made up for this defect. Old traditions, perhaps largely oral, were organized into narrative histories — the stories of the patriarchs, of Moses and Joshua, and of the judges of

Israel. Even more impressive was the vivid and informed contemporary, or near-contemporary, account of David and his mighty men. The reputation of David as a singer and of Solomon as a wise man no doubt attest the cultivation of lyric poetry and gnomic literature under the monarchy; but it is difficult to tell which of the surviving psalms and proverbs may be attributed to this early age.

The historical writing of the Hebrews was infused with the religion of Yahweh, whose hand was seen guiding events. The special role of Yahweh as God of Battles meant that his power manifested itself most distinctly in the military and political sphere. The biblical account of the exodus from Egypt is a striking example of the view that God revealed himself through history. He might indeed show himself as a pillar of smoke by day and of fire by night; but he had revealed himself most tellingly by freeing his people from Pharaoh's bondage.

As a deity directing the course of history, Yahweh was unique in the Middle East. Other war gods were at the same time nature gods — characteristically, as in most ancient Sumer, gods of the storm. Their worship thus easily merged into fertility rites, since the storm not only thundered and destroyed, but also brought rain and new life to vegetation. Not so Yahweh. His worship stood in isolation, emphatically opposed to the religion of the fields. Under the circumstances, old wounds stemming from the initial conflict between a desert God of Battles and the village deities of Canaan could never be entirely healed.

The prophets became the pre-eminent spokesmen for the religion of Yahweh in early Hebrew society. In the time of Saul and David, prophecy was an ecstatic and group phenomenon. Dancing and singing induced trances where were interpreted as signs of direct communion with God; and the men who experienced such trances inspired a reverence which gave them a quasi-sacrosanct status. Their advice was solicited by the community at large whenever matters of import, in which God might be presumed to have an interest, had to be decided.

As spokesmen for Yahweh, the prophets championed his claims to exclusive worship and denounced the cults of Baal. Equally, as spokesmen for the old religion of the desert, they came into conflict with all the newfangled ways of settled society. On the strength of their outward holiness, and sustained by inner conviction, they even dared to attack the monarchy and the unrighteousness of the wealthy and powerful. Thus the prophets served also as specially privileged representatives and spokesmen of the humbler classes in the growingly stratified society of the day.

During the eighth century B.C., the prophetic tradition underwent a great transformation. In place of bands of ecstatic holy men, there arose individual prophets, who felt themselves inspired by Yahweh to denounce social abuses and religious corruption. They did so in fiery poetry. Amos (*ca.* 750 B.C.) was the earliest of these literary prophets whose works have been preserved; but he was quickly followed by Hosea and the first Isaiah. Thereafter, the literary prophetic tradition continued almost unbroken until the time of the author of the Book of Daniel (*ca.* 150 B.C.). These individual prophets inherited at least a share of the mantle of holiness borne by their predecessors. The words of a prophet could never be neglected, not even by kings and priests whose actions the prophet might denounce. The poor and oppressed, whose thoughts and feelings were often given form and direction by the prophets' utterances, no doubt listened eagerly and took seriously the pronouncements made so emphatically in the name of Yahweh, even when immediate events did not always bear out the prophetic foreboding of disaster.

The major theme of the early literary prophets was simple. Yahweh was a just but stern God, who demanded righteous conduct of men and punished those who flouted his commandments. But the Israelites had betrayed their covenant with

Yahweh, forgetting his laws and worshipping false gods. In consequence, disaster was bound to come: a Day of Yahweh, when the sins of the people would be visited upon them and the awful majesty of God revealed to all mankind. The prophets were vague as to exactly what form the Day of Yahweh would take; but many of their prophecies envisioned military and political disaster to the kingdoms of Israel and Judah.

One implication of this view was that Yahweh controlled the destiny not only of his chosen people, but of all mankind. If the Assyrians, for example, overwhelmed the Israelites, it was Yahweh who had summoned the Assyrian armies to punish Israel's sins. Thus the prophets expanded the idea that God revealed himself through history to make him supreme over all the world. In defending and exalting the power of Yahweh, they swept aside the claims of all other divinities and cults and proclaimed monotheism in its clearest and most emphatic form.

But the prophets proclaimed God's justice and mercy as well as his power, arguing that his motive for intervention in human affairs was to safeguard the right and punish evildoing. This juxtaposition of universal power and absolute righteousness brought to a logical culmination the trends toward religious universalism and ethical individualism apparent in other religions of the Middle East during the same centuries. But other peoples, bound by their traditional recognition of a plurality of gods, could not accept monotheism without breaking away from their religious inheritance. Religious thinkers of Israel and Judah were here at an advantage; for the fact that Yahweh had always been a jealous God, hopelessly antagonistic to local fertility cults and demanding an exclusive worship, made the transition to radical monotheism easy. With only a modest reinterpretation of their national religious past, Israel and Judah became uniquely free to develop the full implication of the monotheistic currents of thought already running strongly throughout the Middle East. The Hebrew prophets of the eighth and later centuries exploited their strategic opportunity to the full.

Logic indeed required monotheism. Neither Yahweh nor any other deity or deities could retain a merely local sovereignty in an age when the fate of nations and peoples depended upon the actions of distant Assyria and Egypt. It is improbable that the Hebrew prophets would have asserted their view of God's universal power so clearly and emphatically if such political conditions had not existed. But although the times thus set their mark upon the development of the Hebrew religion, the form of prophetic utterances and the passion with which they were expressed depended upon individual human experience in the context of the Hebrew national religious past.

Interaction between religious and political development was clearly illustrated by the next important stage through which nascent Judaism passed. Political disaster struck in 721 B.C., when the Assyrians overwhelmed the kingdom of Israel and carried many leading families into exile. Under the impress of this apparent fulfilment of prophecy, a party of religious reform arose within the still surviving kingdom of Judah. Nearly a century later, this party came to power when King Josiah (638–609 B.C.) launched an energetic campaign to purify the religion of Yahweh and to repress all traces of other cults. The reformers concentrated the worship of Yahweh at the Temple in Jerusalem and entrusted the rites to priests who sought to conform to the best precedents of ancient and uncorrupted religion. This effort required the collection and codification of all available religious records; and to this enterprise posterity probably owes both the Book of Deuteronomy and the fixation of large parts of the Old Testament into their present form.

But despite the Deuteronomic reforms, Judah was not spared the fate of Israel. King Josiah was barely able to maintain his independence; and almost immediately after his death, the kingdom acknowledged Babylonian overlordship. Then, after a rising inspired in part by prophetic assurances of divine help, King Nebuchadnezzar captured and destroyed Jerusalem (586 B.C.) and deported a large part of the city's population to Babylonia.

The failure of Yahweh to prevent this disaster presented the heirs of the prophetic tradition with a new and formidable challenge. The Deuteronomic reforms had clearly failed to appease God's wrath. What more did God require? What really was his plan? If the religion of Yahweh were to survive, convincing answers to such questions had to be found; for men could not be expected to remain faithful to a God who had inexplicably abandoned them in their hour of need.

In this ultimate crisis, the prophets Ezekiel and the second Isaiah boldly undertook, from their exile in Babylon, to justify the ways of God to man. Ezekiel demanded a still more rigorous obedience to the commands of Yahweh and foresaw as a reward the eventual re-establishment of a united kingdom of Israel and Judah. The fall of Jerusalem he attributed to the survival of pagan and unholy practices even after King Josiah's reforms; and he outlined a still stricter pattern for the future. The second Isaiah, whose eloquent poetry was composed during the lifetime of Cyrus the Great, saw in the Persian victories over Babylon a sure sign that the day was at hand when the sins of Israel would be forgiven and the glory of God become manifest to all the nations. In his view, the sufferings of the Jews were not simply punishment for their disobedience, but part of a far grander divine plan; for when Israel, purged and repentant, had been restored in glory, true religion and just government would be established everywhere. Instead of a petty and persecuted people, exposed to the scorn of more fortunate nations, the children of Israel would take their rightful place as a light to the gentiles and establishers of justice to the ends of the earth.

Such extravagant hopes were of course

never fulfilled; but Ezekiel and the second Isaiah wove a new emotional tone into Judaism. Prophecy in the early days had been largely denunciatory; and the Day of Yahweh had loomed ahead as a time of dreadful doom. Now there was hope — ever delayed but never forgotten — of a Day when, after appropriate and drastic purification, mankind would actually witness the establishment of the Kingdom of God on earth. With eyes fixed confidently on such a future, hardship and disappointment became comparatively easy to bear. Paradoxically, the really pious might even enjoy suffering: indeed, the worse, the better; for in proportion as present afflictions increased in severity, the day of final redress seemed surer and more imminent.

Such eschatological hope was not incompatible with careful elaboration of rules for ritual purity. In the megalopolitan environment of Babylon, such rules were in fact a psychologically very useful substitute for the customary patterning of life in small, homogeneous communities. As a result, the exile community's ritual observances allowed its members to maintain a strong self-consciousness and distinct ethos in the very midst of Babylonia. Moreover, after Cyrus the Persian had overthrown the imperial might of Babylon, and a few Jews began to trickle back to Jerusalem, ritual prescriptions, as elaborated by Ezekiel and others, provided a ready-made blueprint for the new corporate life.

At first the returned exiles, or a party among them, pinned their hope for the restoration of the Kingdom of David upon a layman who claimed descent from the royal house; but this movement soon ran afoul of the Persian authorities and was repressed. Thereafter, the Temple became the principal focus and sole unifying factor for the struggling and precarious Jewish community of Palestine. Not until Nehemiah (ca. 444 B.C.) and Ezra (ca. 397 B.C.) had reorganized the worship of Yahweh at Jerusalem did the community of returned exiles really begin to flourish. Yet this partial success in no way matched the vast expectation built upon the Day of Yahweh; and the hope of its coming remained powerful and ever present, ready to flare into political revolt against alien authority whenever a promising candidate for the role of Messiah — the Lord's anointed — should appear.

Two other aspects of the work of Ezekiel and the second Isaiah need only be mentioned. Ezekiel emphasized, as no predecessor had done, the relation of the individual to God — a response, no doubt, to the weakening of local community solidarity among the exiles in the great cities of Babylonia. This individualization of religious responsibility and observance was pregnant for the future, as was also the second Isaiah's emphasis upon God's fatherly loving-kindness and the patience with which He bore offenses against His will. The stern judge and fiercely jealous God of earlier prophecy was thereby supplemented by a more kindly conception of the Godhead, which merged with the older conceptions in a logically incompatible but psychologically most persuasive fashion.

Thus by 500 B.C., the religion of Yahweh had undergone far-reaching transformations that fitted it to survive as a world religion. Judaism was no longer the cult of a tribe, as in the days of Moses, but a law and doctrine claiming universal validity for itself and total error for all rivals. Moreover, under the exigencies of exile, the worship of Yahweh had survived even without the focus of the Temple at Jerusalem, and without a definite territorial home. Wherever the faithful might gather, prayers, psalms, and reading from the sacred scriptures kept the doctrines and hopes of the Jewish religion alive in the minds and hearts of its adherents. Judaism retained a strong emphasis upon the concept of a chosen people, united to God by a special covenant which set them apart from all others; yet within this collective and corporate frame there developed a belief in direct personal accountancy to God for individual moral and ritual acts.

Both universalism and individualism in

religion were thus accommodated within the national framework which had been inherited from primitive tribal times. As a result, it became possible for men of widely differing modes of life and cultural milieux to remain faithful to the religion of their fathers. Although certain pagan customs were forbidden to the pious, the wide dispersion of later times inevitably led Jews to imitate all sorts of local habits. But such assimilation no longer implied apostasy. Religion had become a separable element in the total cultural complex; and Jews might maintain their faith while in most things taking on the coloring of the society in which they happened to find themselves.

Here was a new phenomenon: a religion which lived a life of its own, largely independent of geographical locality and of secular culture. This is familiar enough in our time and may even seem natural. But by the standard of earlier ages, when religion and the total style of life had been part and parcel of one another — and therefore inseparable from a particular social community living in a more or less fixed geographical location — the new sociological character of Judaism was indeed strange and novel.

The emotional power, poignancy, and literary distinction of the Old Testament need scarcely be emphasized. The poetry of the second Isaiah has seldom been equaled; the same is true of many of the psalms and of such a literary masterpiece as the Book of Job. From an intellectual point of view, revelation manifesting itself in dogmatic assertion and violent denunciation may seem a poor substitute for reasoning; and if modern scholars correctly interpret the intent of prophetic pronouncements, this adverse judgment was also borne out practically, since political prophecies were consistently wrong. Yet the prophets of Israel and Judah struggled hard to solve the dilemma confronting the religious thought of all western Asia: how to justify the apparent injustices and suffering which the Divine imposed even upon righteous men. In Mesopotamia, as we have seen, no solution to this problem was found; and a spirit of religious disillusion gained ground. In Egypt, after the Atonist reform had been repudiated, an increasingly archaic religious formalism prevailed. But in the minds of the Jewish prophets, eager expectation took the place of despair; disappointment intensified rather than weakened religious conviction; and the hope for the coming of the Messiah and of God's kingdom on earth provided a powerful solace in time of trouble.

This conviction, and the magnificent poetry in which it was clothed, have become basic parts of the European cultural inheritance; and one cannot withhold admiration from the men who wrought so enduringly. In an age when the civilization of the Middle East was leveling out toward a flaccid cosmopolitanism, and when dry rot had invaded the two anciently civilized lands of Babylonia and Egypt, the religion and literature of the Jews exhibited an extraordinary power and vigor. In its strong hold over human minds and hearts, uniquely combining religious universalism with individualism and nationalism, lay Judaism's strength and the secret of its future world-transforming career.

SUGGESTIONS FOR ADDITIONAL READING

This bibliography does not include the books from which selections have been taken or which are mentioned in the selection introductions. They should not be overlooked when seeking additional reading matter.

Any of the newer translations of the Bible are suitable for study. Two one-volume editions of the Revised Standard Version are particularly useful: the *Westminster Study Bible* (New York, 1965) and *The Oxford Annotated Bible with the Apocrypha* (New York, 1965).

A number of books are readily available which discuss developments and indicate trends of modern biblical criticism, among them H. H. Rowley, *The Growth of the Old Testament* (London, 1950), and *The Old Testament and Modern Study* (Oxford, 1951). There are two one-volume biblical dictionaries which are recommended: *Dictionary of the Bible*, edited by James Hastings, revised edition by Frederick C. Grant and H. H. Rowley (New York, 1963), and John L. McKenzie, S.J., *Dictionary of the Bible* (Milwaukee, 1965). The student will also find that a biblical atlas can be a most valuable tool. One of the best is G. Ernest Wright and Floyd V. Filson, *The Westminster Historical Atlas to the Bible* (rev. ed., New York, 1956).

Jack Finegan's *Light from the Ancient Past* (Princeton, 1946) is an excellent study of the relationship between the history of the ancient Near East and the Bible. In a similar vein are two books edited by James B. Pritchard, *Ancient Near Eastern Texts Relating to the Old Testament* (2nd ed., Princeton, 1956) and *The Ancient Near East in Pictures Relating to the Old Testament* (Princeton, 1954). Students will also find that much valuable information is contained in a standard text, Bernard W. Anderson, *Understanding the Old Testament* (2nd ed., Englewood Cliffs,

N. J., 1966). Anderson's bibliography is especially complete. Another book which illuminates the Old Testament is Samuel Sandmell, *The Hebrew Scriptures: An Introduction to Their Literature and Religious Ideas* (New York, 1963).

A collection of essays in honor of William Foxwell Albright edited by G. Ernest Wright, *The Bible and the Ancient Near East* (New York, 1961), will throw added light on many of the subjects discussed in this volume. Some of the authors represented here made contributions to this collection. Moreover the volume contains a bibliography of Albright's work.

John Bright's *A History of Israel* (Philadelphia, 1959), and Robinson H. Wheeler's *The History of Israel* (London, 1957), are both better-than-average standard histories. The same subject is covered in W. F. Albright's excellent brief survey, *The Biblical Period From Abraham to Ezra* (New York, 1963). For additional information about Israel's neighbors the student may turn to S. Moscati, *The Face of The Ancient Orient* (Garden City, N. Y., 1962), G. Roux, *Ancient Iraq* [Mesopotamia] (Harmondsworth, England, 1966), H. W. F. Saggs, *The Greatness That Was Babylon* (London, 1962), J. Breasted, *A History of Egypt* (New York, 1909), and G. Steindorff and K. C. Seele, *When Egypt Ruled the East* (2nd ed., Chicago, 1957).

A book which looks at the history of the Jewish patriarchs in the light of recent archaeological discoveries is John Holt, *The Patriarchs of Israel* (Nashville, 1964).

Moses is the subject of a suggestive study which is less concerned with the issue of monotheism than it is with other aspects of his story: Gerhard von Rad's *Moses* (London, 1960).

Dennis J. McCarthy, S.J., *Treaty and Covenant, a Study in the Ancient Oriental Documents and in the Old Testament* (Rome, 1963), explores the relationship between the form of Hittite treaties and that of Israel's covenant. A related study is that of Murray Lee Newman, Jr., *The People of the Covenant: A Study of Israel from Moses to the Monarchy* (New York, 1962).

Sigmund Freud's excursions into history and religion include *Totem and Taboo, The Future of an Illusion,* and of course *Moses and Monotheism.* These are best read in *The Standard Edition of The Complete Psychological Works of Sigmund Freud,* ed. J. Strachey, 23 vols. (London, 1953–1966), but they are also available singly in various editions and translations. These writings are analyzed in psychological terms in David Bakan's *Sigmund Freud and the Jewish Mystical Tradition* (Princeton, 1959). Ernest Jones offers a favorable appraisal of *Moses and Monotheism* in *The Life and Work of Sigmund Freud,* Vol. 3: *The Last Phase, 1919–1939* (New York, 1957).

Though the books listed above have generally been cited in their hardback editions, many of them — and many more that might have been included here — are now available in paperback editions.

1 2 3 4 5 6 7 8 9 10